THE BASICS OF BUSINESS START-UP

The Basics of Business Start-Up outlines the entrepreneurial journey from inception to start-up. Starting from the basic concepts and working through the start-up process step by step, the book is an indispensable guide both for would-be entrepreneurs and students on entrepreneurship/small business courses.

Key features of this book include:

- A step-by-step, sequential approach, detailing the typical entrepreneurial journey.
- Non-technical introduction to the basic business functions, including budgeting, accounting, marketing, and more.
- A readable and accessible beginner's guide to entrepreneurship and business start-up.

Written in a refreshingly personal style, this concise guide is the perfect starting point for anyone seeking to put their entrepreneurial ambitions into action.

Alexandrina Pauceanu has extensive international experience in teaching, consulting, and mentoring students for developing new businesses. Currently, she is Professor at Open Institute of Technology Malta and Chair of the Examination Board at The Entrepreneurship Academy. She also mentors junior researchers through the EURAXESS program.

THE BASICS OF BUSINESS START-UP

Alexandrina Pauceanu

Routledge
Taylor & Francis Group
LONDON AND NEW YORK

Designed cover image: Getty Images © Credit: Designer.

First published 2026
by Routledge
4 Park Square, Milton Park, Abingdon, Oxon OX14 4RN

and by Routledge
605 Third Avenue, New York, NY 10158

Routledge is an imprint of the Taylor & Francis Group, an informa business

British Library Cataloguing-in-Publication Data
A catalogue record for this book is available from the British Library

ISBN: 978-1-032-96953-4 (hbk)
ISBN: 978-1-032-96952-7 (pbk)
ISBN: 978-1-003-59142-9 (ebk)

DOI: 10.4324/9781003591429

Typeset in Bembo
by Apex CoVantage, LLC

CONTENTS

INTRODUCTION

What if everything you've been told about entrepreneurship is a lie?

You've heard the myth: 'Build it, and they will come.' But here's the truth – 82% of startups fail because founders skip the gritty, unglamorous work of laying solid business foundations. I've seen brilliant ideas collapse because entrepreneurs rushed into markets without validating demand. Others burned through cash, ignoring financial discipline, or underestimated competitors by relying solely on passion and hustle. These aren't rare exceptions – they're common pitfalls for those who leap before looking.

This book isn't about inspiration. It's about preparation.

Think of me as your strategic advisor. Over 12 years, I've guided entrepreneurs from Dubai's dynamic free zones to Europe's competitive startup ecosystems. What separates thriving ventures from failed dreams? Three powerful pillars:

- **Strategies that scale** (we'll craft business models competitors envy)
- **Systems that sustain growth** (your future self will thank you)
- **Networks that amplify your impact** (even when you're sleeping)

Notice I didn't say 'vision' or 'grind.' Those come after you've built resilient foundations. Here's your first test: Can you spot the fatal flaw in this startup pitch?

'Our product is so innovative it has no competition.'
(If you shrugged, Chapter 3 will save your business.)

DOI: 10.4324/9781003591429-1

Throughout this journey, we'll dissect real-world startup mistakes and rebuild smarter. You'll leverage FabLab prototypes, master AI-driven marketing strategies, optimize cash flow management, and future-proof your venture before your first sale.

Warning: This isn't motivational fluff. By the end of this book, you'll automate tedious tasks, validate market demand rigorously, and possess what 97% of founders lack – a clear roadmap for sustainable success.

Still reading? Good.

Your competitors aren't.

1

THE RESILIENT LAUNCHPAD

From self-awareness to startup success

75% of startups fail. But here's the secret: Most collapse because founders skip this part.

It is a good idea to start a business venture while you are working (as a secondary activity). There is usually the feeling of being one's own boss and the freedom attached to it. Not to be forgotten is the financial liberty an entrepreneur dreams of daily. All these make the possibility of being an entrepreneur attractive and alluring.

However, becoming a successful entrepreneur takes more than a simple desire. There are many obstacles and challenges that must be overcome to have a measure of success. What are some of these challenges? What can an entrepreneur do to overcome them? These and many other issues related to having a successful business will be the focus of discussion in this chapter. But first, let us understand what qualifies someone as an entrepreneur.

There are different definitions for the term 'entrepreneur.' However, these few definitions sum up what qualifies a person to be regarded as an entrepreneur. First, an entrepreneur is an individual who initiates a business idea, runs it, takes risks, and takes responsibility for either the success or failure of the business venture.

An entrepreneur is also commonly referred to as the person who, instead of working for others, decides to start and run a personal business, taking all the risks, making the decisions, and taking the credit for the success or otherwise of the business or company.

DOI: 10.4324/9781003591429-2

According to M.J. Gottlieb, a successful businessman and the author of the book *How to Ruin a Business Without Really Trying* (Morgan James Publishing, 2014), 'an entrepreneur is someone who can take any idea, whether it be a product/service, and have the skill set, will and courage to take extreme risks to do whatever it takes to turn that concept into reality and not only bring it to market, but make it a viable product and/or service that people want or need.'

The entrepreneurship endeavor is a journey, and it is not an easy one. It comes with satisfactions and downfalls, small and/or big successes and road bumps, and the unknown. Are you ready for all of it?

You need to ask yourself if you really want to start this journey and are motivated enough to lead through the way. If your answer is yes, what does it take to become a successful entrepreneur? Before we discuss that, let's consider how to find the right business opportunity.

The first and most important thing is to know your motivation behind starting the business. This step is essential, as sometimes, during the process, you might need a reminder of why you are doing this. You can either choose a motivation from the following list or write yours at the end of the list:

1. Become independent – work at your own pace, work for yourself, and work from anywhere and anytime.
2. Personal satisfaction – you are the only one responsible for achieving your key performance indicators (KPIs). Even if you work long hours in the beginning, the result should keep you on track.
3. Financial freedom – gain money to afford the lifestyle and the freedom you want.
4. Choose your team – you have the flexibility to choose the people you want to work with (employees or freelancers).
5. Invest in yourself, your skills, and your future – you decide which courses to take and when and which skills to develop and select your own key performance indicators. A KPI is a measurable indicator used to evaluate the success of a project, an employee, or a firm.
6. Build your personal brand – and become the brand. Building a brand is not an easy thing. It starts with you, the entrepreneur, and your values and motivations.

MY reason(s) for starting my own enterprise is/are:

1. ______________________________
2. ______________________________
3. ______________________________
4. ______________________________

Identifying the WHY will help you stay on track, and these notes will be a good reminder of your motivation and initial plans.

The next step is to find an activity that fits the following criteria: You have deep knowledge about it, you like it, and you can make money out of it (there is demand on the market). To justify these three criteria, please note that if you do not like what you do, it will become a burden and lead you to failure. If you do not have deep knowledge about it, you should get it before starting (either by taking some specialized courses; practicing in the field; or working for 6 to 12 months to gain experience, knowledge, and specific insights).

INSTRUCTIONS FOR FILLING IN TABLE 1: FINDING YOUR 'SWEET SPOT' FOR MONEY MAKING

Areas/activities of deep knowledge/experience – these are activities/areas in which you are skilled and have extensive knowledge and/or experience. For example, cooking, testing applications, handcrafting, repairing things, talking with people, or building websites.

Areas/activities one enjoys practicing – these are activities you enjoy doing/practicing even if you do not have experience or deep knowledge. It could be dancing, reading, crafting, advising on fashion, or translating, among many other examples.

Areas/activities that can be monetized – you need to examine the first two columns and see if there are common denominators. If yes, think of those skills that can be monetized in real life and how. If you identify some activities that you enjoy and can be monetized, but you do not have enough knowledge and/or experience, do not despair. It is time to act and gain the knowledge and experience required. You could start with an online free course or available materials, gain an internship in a company with similar activities, or become an employee for 6 to 12 months in an organization with similar activities.

The next obvious question is this: What if there is an activity in the knowledge column that can be monetized, but I do not like/ enjoy it? Then, my best advice is not to go for it; it will be a failure and feel like a burden to carry out. Instead, keep looking until you find the activity that you like; can gain knowledge and experience in; and, most importantly, can capitalize (monetize) on.

To obtain a clear perspective, please fill in the following table. Once filled in, reflect on it and see what you need to do to identify an area that meets the three requirements. Is there any area/activity in all three columns? If yes, how can you monetize it? Think broadly and assess all the options you might think of.

Table 1.1 No-BS money maker matrix

No.	Areas/Activities of Deep Knowledge/ Experience	Areas/Activities That One Enjoys	Areas/Activities That Can Be Monetized

Red Flag Alert: If your 'Areas/Activities of Deep Knowledge/Experience' and 'Areas/ Activities That One Enjoys' columns don't overlap, STOP. Monetizing misery = guaranteed burnout.

Personal development is essential for a successful entrepreneur, even if it is just a brush-up on knowledge. It goes hand in hand with professional development. And we should not forget the most important thing: Take care of yourself physically and mentally. Take time and disconnect, spend time with loved ones, and enjoy life.

Real constraints are those that really exist, usually in a limited quantity and independent of our influence. The most common real constraints in an entrepreneurial journey are resources (human capital, products, knowledge, technology, own skills, knowledge), time, and money. The not-so-real constraints usually start with 'I can't do it because . . .'

From experience, I have seen people finding excuses for themselves almost automatically for not starting or for not following through. Whenever a sentence begins with 'I try/tried to . . .,' 'I will try to . . .,' 'I will give it a try . . .,' or 'I will see what I can do for . . .,' it is a clear reason not to do things. Therefore, an important part of your personal development is to give up these and replace them with winning words: 'I am doing this,' 'I am implementing the strategies . . .,' 'I am doing it,' 'I got this,' and so on.

REMEMBER: Find reasons to DO things, not for not doing them. In this way, you will adopt a winner's mindset.

Now, reflect on situations where you wanted to do things but ended up not doing them. What was the reason? Is it a real constraint or a not-so-real one?

In terms of partnerships (suppliers, employees, freelancers, customers),[1] one should regard and handle them in win-win situations (where all the involved parties have fair benefits from the transaction). When crafting a proposal or strategy, you can use Table 1.2 to list the wins of your partnership. Whenever you craft a sales pitch or strategy, you will need to focus on your partner's wins, gains, and needs.[2]

A SWOT analysis is a synthesis of your (or your firm's) strong points, weak points, opportunities, and threats. The main purpose of such an analysis is to make yourself aware of all the factors related to your business so you can make informed decisions about what to do next. A SWOT analysis can also be done before starting a business; it will help the investor to assess the pluses and minuses and act on them. Typically, after a SWOT analysis comes an action plan focused on converting weaknesses into strengths, ways

Table 1.2 Assessing the partnership with ____

Points for Negotiation	My Wins	Partner's Wins	What Can I Offer in Addition to Sweeten the Deal?

Note: Wins could be, for example, a long-term supplier at competitive rates, quality raw materials or products, or joint projects. For the supplier, wins could be a long-term customer, referrals, the possibility to use the feedback for marketing purposes, or the opportunity for joint research or projects.

to take advantage of identified opportunities, and ways to handle the identified threats. A personal SWOT analysis is recommended every year, while for businesses, it is recommended during major decision-making, mostly related to growth, expansion, or new product development or commercialization.

As an entrepreneur, you should perform skills assessments every year and continuously work to become a better version of yourself. The only realistic term of comparison is you from the previous period (you now versus you last year, last month, and so on).

Now is the time to make your own SWOT analysis. Take your time and be objective. It is also recommended to involve people you trust so you can have a broader perspective. SWOT analysis is a good tool to assess yourself, compare progress from a period of time to another, and remind yourself of options. A SWOT analysis without an action plan is useless. And, of course, the action plan must be implemented.

Once you honestly identify your weaknesses, it is important to create an action plan to work on transforming them into strengths or diminishing the impact they might have on your personal or professional life. It is recommended to set a date for revision, so you can evaluate the situation and determine what might further be needed.

Table 1.3 SWOT analysis of_______

Date:

Own Strengths (S)	Opportunities (Externals) (O)	Own Weaknesses (W)	Threats (Externals) (T)

Notes for SWOT analysis: Strengths and weaknesses are strictly related to our persona; these could be a lack of time management skills (W), good people management skills (S), or fierce competition (T), for example.

Table 1.4 Action plan template

No.	Activity From SWOT	Corrective Measure(s)	Deadline	Additional Info

Notes for the action plan: The purpose is to plan and organize corrective activities or measures based on the elements of the SWOT analysis. For example, if in the weaknesses column of the SWOT analysis, one identifies that they lack digital marketing knowledge, a corrective measure could be taking one or more digital marketing courses with practical knowledge. In the additional info section, one might add additional details for the task or activity (supplier of the training; person in charge of the activity in business situations; specific website links; related costs, if any).

Let's examine the new skills needed to succeed nowadays during the entrepreneurial journey in a digital world:

1. *Financial management* – this skill is the foundation for your further development. After all, if one can't properly manage their income (or salary), how can they manage a firm's finances? Financial management requires a budget, expense tracking (either via an app or an Excel sheet), and savings (at least 10% of the income at the beginning, and the amount should be

increased with time).[3] You can use these savings for your sunny or rainy days and in the firm for unforeseen situations that might arise. It must be noted here that one should assess available insurance policies and get insured for specific risks personally or in business. This skill can be developed with practice by taking courses and/or reading financial education books or blogs.

2. *General management abilities* – the fundamental four principles of management (planning, organizing, implementing, and control evaluation) are essential in any activity. Based on these, one can further develop managerial skills (such as project management, time management, marketing management, and money management).
3. *Time management* – another vital skill for an entrepreneur. One can try various ways and find the one that best suits one's particular situation. A general agenda app for the smartphone is an excellent tool for keeping track of tasks, scheduling meetings, and planning for upcoming days. Setting up productivity targets for the allotted time is essential and contributes to one's progress. It will help you have small wins, keep track of your priorities, and achieve your goals in the end.
4. *Effective communication* – effective communication starts with active listening. This statement might seem strange, but it is accurate. Active listening can be defined as listening with full attention, understanding exactly what is being said,[4] and providing a meaningful reply or contribution to the discussion. Another important element of effective communication is empathy. These skills can be developed through practice. Effective communication is also essential while managing people, selling products and services, or pitching your business idea to investors or stakeholders.[5]
5. *People management* – working with people is the most challenging and, one might say, difficult task because people are unique, diverse, and different from each other. Empathy and effective communication are important elements in team management, as well as respect, constructive feedback, achievable KPIs, and clear professional development and career track. Investing in your team (time, money, and effort) will transform them from human resources into human capital. This skill can

be developed through practice, human interactions, and end-of-the-day analysis of these activities. Usually, when an entrepreneur needs to make decisions affecting the whole business, they should consider a holistic approach and decide accordingly (humane entrepreneurship).

6. *Specific knowledge* related to the activity domain – it comes as a mandatory requirement for one's success. Knowing the subterfuges, common issues, and specificities will grant you a competitive advantage.
7. *Basic accounting notions*[6] – such as breakeven point, cost calculation, debit and credit, variable and fixed costs, sale price calculation, and budget setting and management.
8. *Marketing and digital marketing knowledge* – the fundamental of marketing is the 4Ps (price, product, place, and promotion). Whenever we plan a marketing strategy, we need to consider all these components to be effective. There is a prevalent digital 'push,' and companies must adapt to survive and be competitive.
9. *Networking skills* – networking is defined as interacting with other partners to develop professional contacts and/or exchange information. We can separate networking into two categories: networking for ideas (discussing your business challenges with people who are different from you in terms of gender, education, experience, profession, and cultural background to get new ideas or perspectives) and networking to develop professional contacts to be used for business purposes (acquisitions, services, suppliers, joint venturing). Networking is an essential part of business and contributes to achieving its KPIs.
10. *Personal branding* – at the beginning of the journey, YOU are the brand and the business card of your idea. Personal and professional development, social media, engaging in activities with an impact on the community, giving back, and communicating with the shareholders become a responsibility and a must. Digital marketing knowledge will be of great help here as well. People do business with other people.
11. *Business automation for specific tasks* – with the recent technological boost, a plethora of tools became available to entrepreneurs to relieve them of certain time-consuming or repetitive tasks. We can utilize diverse programs, from automatic booking systems for meetings and sessions (Appointy, Setmore, Calendly,

Google meetings) and online meeting tools (Google Meet, Teams, Zoom, Skype) to project management tools, automatic postings for social media, integrated billing and accounting applications, and many more. Practically, you might find applications for almost everything with automation potential in business.

12. *Emotion management* – when it is a matter of business, one should learn to control emotions. An *emotions journal*[7] can be used to identify situations and reactions to certain situations. This way, one becomes aware and can react much better to stressful or difficult situations. Also, if you do business with your family, it is highly recommended to separate work occurrences from family time and situations.
13. *Local market knowledge* – this is essential, as you should know the socio-economic and cultural aspects of the country/region you are in. You can use the Hofstede Cultural Compass[8] to gain insights or compare countries in terms of cultural aspects. Other well-documented resources include National Institute of Statistics reports, National or Central Bank, ministries, international consultancy companies' reports (such as KPMG and Deloitte), industry associations or interest groups, and Google trends. An entrepreneur or investor should dedicate at least 20 minutes daily to keeping up with events in their sector locally and globally; one can select trustable resources of information or read the latest research.
14. Digital and AI skills[9] – entrepreneurs must treat AI tools as *amplifiers* of their unique value, not replacements for human ingenuity. For instance, **Jasper AI** can draft marketing copy in seconds, but pairing it with your brand's storytelling (e.g., a bakery owner adding artisanal baking anecdotes to AI-generated social posts) creates differentiation. Similarly, **Pega AI**'s predictive analytics can forecast market trends, enabling proactive pivots – like identifying the 2025 surge in eco-conscious consumers and launching biodegradable packaging before competitors react. However, relying solely on generic AI tools risks blending into the crowd. Differentiation emerges when you *combine* AI efficiency with your 'sweet spot' (Table 1.1). A tech founder might use **Perplexity AI** to analyze Failure CV patterns, uncovering niche solutions competitors overlook, while a

consultant could deploy **Venngage**'s AI-driven cultural insights (Hofstede's Compass) to tailor branding for regional markets.

With 75% of small businesses now using AI tools, standing out requires strategic adoption. Automate *repetitive tasks* (e.g., **Calendly** for scheduling, **Zapier** for workflows) to reclaim 10–15 hours weekly, but reserve creativity for trend anticipation. For example, **Notion AI**'s data analysis can highlight rising demand for AI-augmented coaching – prompting a leadership trainer to launch hybrid human–AI mentorship programs. Staying ahead means treating AI as a co-pilot: let it handle logistics while you focus on *interpretation* (e.g., transforming **ChatGPT** market research into hyper-personalized customer journeys).

The entrepreneurial mindset allows you to identify business opportunities and make the most out of them, learn and overcome failure or setbacks, and be successful in various situations. The knowledge and tools presented in this guide are meant to provide the foundation for an entrepreneurial mindset upon which you will continue to build. Some ways to further refine your entrepreneurial mindset could be:

1. Be curious[10] in business and ask WHY five times – to understand the root cause or uncover hidden insights (Why did A happen? Because of B; Why did B happen? Because of C, and so on).
2. Set clear and measurable goals – this way, you can monitor whether you are on track and whether you achieved your goal. Once achieved, enjoy the small or not-so-small wins.
3. Redefine failure as a learning experience – analyze the situation objectively, see what went well and not so well, and learn from it. Then, next time, you can do much better.
4. Create value for your firm, employees, and, most importantly, your customers. A company, product, or service can't exist without customers. So, you need to be clear right from the planning phase: What value are you offering your customers (perceived value)? Why should the customers buy from you? How do you differentiate from the competition? Why now? How will you keep up with the changes and competition? Innovation is the implementation of your creativity or creative

ideas; a product/service/process can be considered innovative as long as someone is willing to pay for it (because it meets a need that needs to be fulfilled).

5. Face your fears – the most common fear is the one related to business failure. Whenever I discuss this with my customers, my first question is, 'What is the worst thing that can happen if you fail in business?' And the answers might vary from 'I would feel sad' and 'My friends will think of me as useless' to 'I get disappointed and angry.' My follow-up question is, 'So what?' and the conversation partners remain somehow surprised – I see that many of them have that a-ha moment when they realize that things are not as bad as they imagined. Then, my next question is, 'Can you start over?' Most of the answers are 'Yes, I can.' For those who answer 'No,' my next question is, 'Why?' To continue, my next question is, 'What can you do better this time?' or 'What have you learned from this experience?' I do recommend answering such questions in writing.

One recently developed approach to failure is called the Failure CV. The concept of a 'Failure CV' or 'Résumé of Failures' has gained traction in recent years, challenging traditional notions of success and professional development. This unconventional approach to documenting one's career journey offers valuable insights into personal growth, resilience, and the true nature of achievement. A Failure CV serves multiple functions:

1. It provides a more balanced view of an individual's professional journey.
2. It normalizes setbacks and failures as part of the learning process.
3. It shows resilience and the capability of learning from mistakes.
4. It creates a culture of transparency and authenticity in professional circles.

The next question is what a Failure CV should contain. The minimum sections I recommend are: rejected job applications, unsuccessful projects undertaken, business ventures that did not work, proposals or pitches not taken, academic failure (e.g., paper rejection, course failure), relationship failure. Each entry should be followed by a personal reflection of lessons learned and subsequent growth. The sections should be selected based on the purpose of the Failure CV: either professional or personal.

The next imminent question is why. Why should we craft such a CV?

1. *Personal Growth:* 'Documenting failures' encourages self-reflection, which can help in discovering a pattern in decision-making or an area of improvement. Self-awareness is always necessary for long-term professional development.
2. *Organizational Culture:* The culture of a Failure CV can help create a more open and innovative workplace environment. If the leadership can actually show where they have failed, it creates an atmosphere of risk-taking and learning from failure.
3. *Hiring Practices:* To recruiters and hiring managers, a Failure CV may provide deeper insight into the character, resilience, and problem-solving abilities of an applicant.

While the concept has its merits, there is a flip side to consider, specifically the misconception by those who don't know what a Failure CV is. These include risk of overshooting by revealing too much or focusing on the negative side and risk of discrimination if not put in context. On how to make such a Failure CV meaningful and useful, some practical tips could be the following:

1. Group failures into categories: job applications, academic, business ventures, or personal.
2. Provide relevant details: Each entry should contain a short description, date, or time period and context.
3. Focus on significant events: Emphasize major setbacks or failures that had a significant effect on personal or professional growth.
4. Be specific: Give specific examples and not general statements, which can make your Failure CV more poignant and relatable.
5. Identify lessons learned: Clearly define what was learned from each of these failures and how that helped in personal or professional growth.

6. Analyze for patterns: With multiple failures, identify if there are underlying themes or trends that allow deep insight into your decision processes.
7. Showcase growth: Relate how those lessons from previously experienced failures have contributed toward subsequent successes.
8. Keep them short: However much you want to write, in as concise detail as possible, maintain reader interest.
9. Use a clear layout: Set up your Failure CV with headers, bullet points, and consistent formatting for easy readability.
10. Keep it up to date: The Failure CV is a living document; add new entries and insights as you experience them.

What would be the practical applications and purpose in real life of such an exercise?

1. Personal development: Your Failure CV could serve as a reference point of self-reflection and mapping how much you have grown over time.
2. Interview preparation: Refer to this for responding to some frequently asked questions about how difficulties have been overcome or what mistakes you learned from.
3. Team building: Share some of these previously mentioned entries in your Failure CV with workgroup members for developing an open, resilient organizational culture.
4. Mentorship: Allow your Failure CV to mentor and inspire others that one faces setbacks along the way to any successful career.

The Failure CV is a paradigm shift in our approach toward professional development and success. Embracing failures and learning from them begets a far more honest, resilient, and growth-oriented approach to careers. Implementation, though, should be thoughtful and contextual to maximize benefits while minimizing potential risks.

Another approach to failure is to work on your mindset, and a good start is to answer the following questions:

1. What is your definition of failure in your business? How will you know you have partially or totally failed?
2. What is the worst thing that can happen if you fail in business or some aspects of business?
3. How can you handle the responses from Point 2? Mitigation?
4. Can/would you start over again? Why or why not?
5. What can you do better this time? What have you learned from this experience?
6. Can you replace 'I can't because . . .,' 'I won't succeed because . . .,' or similar beliefs with 'I can because . . .' and 'I will succeed because . . .'? I would suggest writing these new beliefs down in the following or in a notebook.

Let's be blunt: Fear will whisper, 'What if you fail?' Let it. Then ask back: 'What if I don't try?' Every entrepreneur's journey is paved with moments where courage drowns doubt – not by ignoring risks but by preparing for them. Those AI tools and digital platforms we've discussed? Treat them like your 2025 secretary: affordable, reliable, and quietly revolutionary. They'll automate invoices while you innovate, schedule meetings while you strategize, and analyze trends while you sleep. But remember – tools don't build empires; *you* do. Your SWOT analysis sharpens your edge. Your Failure CV fuels resilience. Now, reread your 'Why.' Tape it where you'll see it daily. Entrepreneurship isn't about fearless leaps – it's about calculated steps forward, even when your knees shake. The road ahead? It's yours to shape. Start today. Iterate tomorrow. Repeat.

NOTES

1 In practice, frequently the term customer is used interchangeably with the term consumer. In this book, we do differentiate between these two terms. The customer is the person who is buying a product or a service, while the consumer is the end user of the product or the service. Of course, a customer can also be a consumer if the purchase is for their own use.

2 The partner's needs may vary depending on the relationship you have. For example, increasing sales by 10% in the next 12 months, job security for employees, setting the price and quality of the product or service so that they are highly competitive for your customers, and so on.

3 Simply saving money will not bring you prosperity. Savings are usually affected by inflation if kept in a bank account, and typically, bank interest rates don't even cover the inflation rate. It is recommended to keep your emergency fund (cost of expenses for six months) and 'oxygen line' (total expenses for 6–12 months) in financial instruments that can be easily accessed (bank or savings accounts, government bonds, etc.). Saving without investing will not give you the desired result, and for these, you should put your money into circulation. Invest in a rental studio apartment, in the stock market, in government bonds, in gold, in art, and so on, depending on your risk appetite and personal situation. A business is an investment.
4 Listening with full attention means being present, both physically and mentally, in the conversation. Our conversation partner will notice if we are not present. It's important to note that physical and mental presence in a conversation is an integral part of charisma.
5 A stakeholder is defined as a person or entity that has a direct or indirect interest in your company. Stakeholders can be suppliers, customers, the government, shareholders, and so on.
6 This extensive knowledge facilitates your ability to put things into perspective, knowing what to ask from your accountant, marketer, employees, and so on. The demand for results should be made in a measurable way, taking into account the KPIs or indicators that you agree upon.
7 The emotion journal is a practical tool for identifying, becoming aware of, and controlling emotions. This journal involves describing situations that have generated a less-desired reaction/emotion and identifying the stimulus. By being aware of the factors that determine emotions, we can learn to control our reactions/emotions. It's important to understand that the only thing within our power to control is our way of reacting/responding to a particular situation.
8 You can visit the following website to get more resources on this topic: www.theculturefactor.com/country-comparison-tool
9 To stay ahead of the competition in a very competitive and volatile business environment, it is mandatory to keep up with digital tool development and even go for at least a hybrid business model.
10 Nevertheless, I recommend you be curious while maintaining certain boundaries and not invading a person's intimate space without their consent. Typically, participants in research studies sign an informed consent form, and the consent can be withdrawn at any moment.

2

PROFIT AND PURPOSE

Aligning your business with humanity's core needs

What if the daily frustration that kept Sheila Lirio Marcelo awake at 3 AM became a $1.3B empire? From McDonald's 69-million-customer secret to pandemic-proof strategies, this chapter decodes how to mine pain points – yours or your neighbor's – into goldmines, using Maslow's playbook to build businesses the future can't ignore.

It is critical that you find the right business opportunity for you, and it should match the criteria previously discussed.[1] This may seem easier said than done, but the following tips will guide you in the right direction.

ALWAYS STUDY YOUR ENVIRONMENT FOR POSSIBLE OPPORTUNITIES

One of the facts that we usually ignore is that our environment abounds with many business opportunities. If you can take the time to find out what people lack in your neighborhood or area, you can address that lack and turn it into a business opportunity. Let us consider a typical example.

In 1940, two brothers, Richard and Maurice, saw the need for the people in their neighborhood to have a decent restaurant to care for their needs. They pooled resources together and opened a restaurant in San Bernardino, California, United States. Today, that little restaurant serves almost 68 million people daily. The customers are scattered over 119 different countries and fed by over 36,000 outlets

DOI: 10.4324/9781003591429-3

covering many continents. With nearly 2 million employees, it ranks behind Walmart as the largest employer of labor in the world. Welcome to the world of McDonald's. Those two McDonald brothers got the business idea when they looked for what the people needed. They exploited this lack to build a business empire that rakes in millions of dollars annually. McDonald's wouldn't have achieved such success if those brothers didn't look inward for business opportunities.

STUDY EXISTING BUSINESS IDEAS

Wherever you turn, there are existing businesses that are solving people's problems. You can use these business ideas as your case study. How can you do that? What can you do better or different from them? Analyze whichever one catches your fancy. Study how this business idea solves people's problems and the potential challenges the business owner faces. Take time to find out the shortcomings of this enterprise that the customers want to see addressed. You can use this information to start a different business entirely or start a similar business with the objective of blocking those loopholes and addressing such shortcomings.

We all know that Disneyland's Magic Kingdom is one of the most adventurous places to be in the world. How was the idea of this awesome amusement park conceived? Walt Disney and his family went on a vacation to Tivoli Gardens, one of the best in the world. He studied the park and concluded that he could do something better when he returned home. So, he came back to California to establish his own amusement park without wasting much time. To give his visitors a lasting experience there, he built on the foundation of Tivoli Gardens and worked on the shortcomings of the old park. What is the result? We now have a world-class park that can compete with any other in the world. So, look at what others are doing that you feel you can do better and pursue your dream of making it a success.

Every successful enterprise offers lessons. Walt Disney visited Copenhagen's Tivoli Gardens in 1951 but saw room for improvement. He added:

- Themed zones for immersive storytelling.
- Character meet-and-greets.
- Family-friendly amenities.

The result? Disneyland became the world's most-visited theme park, welcoming 18 million guests annually.

What can you do now? Start with the identification of top three competitors in your field and analyze their 1-star online reviews for common complaints. Then build solutions to address their weakest points.

Pro Tip: 63% of customers switch brands due to poor service – fix what others overlook!

THINK ABOUT THE FUTURE

The world is changing so fast that one needs special grace and attention to keep pace. If you want a good business idea, you will do yourself a lot of good if you can pretend that the future is here. This is important since some of the business opportunities today may become obsolete and absolutely irrelevant in the near future. For instance, the advent of technology has opened a new chapter in the history of the world. This is what many people like Bill Gates and Steve Jobs saw when they started their computer-making companies some decades ago. Today, what will happen when driverless cars take over human-driven cars? Are there opportunities in this? Aside from this, think of what you believe people living in the future can't do without. For instance, will people be able to do without mobile devices, computers, and others? You can start planning for the future now by putting the necessary machinery in place to tap these future opportunities. When the future is really here, you will have set yourself on the path of becoming a world changer and shaker. Bill and Steve did that and are now respected throughout the world. The legacy that Steve Jobs left behind will remain relevant for years to come. You can take a page from these investors' books with good insight.

Digitization of businesses has quickly become a reality, and organizations are still adapting to it, from digital tools for working from home to completely digital shops and offices. Before the COVID-19 pandemic, companies were reluctant to have people working away from their offices. However, with the Great Resignation in progress now, they need to find ways to retain talent while keeping control and managing costs.

SOLVE A PERSONAL PROBLEM

Some investors started off by addressing their personal problems. They did this when they couldn't find solutions to particular problems they faced. They realized that since there was nobody with a solution to that problem, they themselves could be the solution. For instance, let's consider the case of Sheila Lirio Marcelo. Sheila founded Care.com to solve some personal problems.

A couple of years ago, Sheila's father underwent surgery three times. Sheila and her husband were working full-time and had two little kids and two dogs to take care of. At one point, she wanted a website that could help her handle some of her numerous demands of taking care of her sick father, helping her kids, and working her job. She tried looking for a solution on the internet but didn't come up with something helpful. Since she didn't want to hire personal nannies or pet sitters because of unforeseen occurrences, she became helpless.

Sheila saw this as an opportunity and started her company, Care.com, in 2006 to provide adequate services for individuals who need support for their pets, children, elderly parents, and tutoring. What is the result? She has used her platform to keep many women in the corporate world by providing the needed assistance to keep their jobs. Now, Care.com has millions of members (about 33 million in 2019) in 20 countries. Before the company went public in 2014, it had raised over $100 million. Sheila solved her personal problem and became an entrepreneur in the process. Is that not wonderful? What stops you from doing the same?

MAKE GOOD USE OF THE INTERNET AND AI TOOLS

The internet remains the biggest source of business opportunities in the world. If you are short of business ideas, check the internet. Nearly all the sectors of the world economy have business opportunities for individuals to avail themselves of. If you are interested in online business, there are many opportunities, such as blogging, vlogging, e-marketing, and other freelance jobs. If you are not interested in online business, there are many different business ideas that you can implement without much stress. So, don't just sit down and do nothing; pick up your PC and surf the web. The number of business suggestions will surprise you.

Social media is another good resource for business ideas. There are many groups of entrepreneurs, freelancers, mothers, or parents where you can get insights, study their needs[2] and complaints, and test potential ideas you might have for that particular market segment. For example, platforms like LinkedIn's AI Opportunity Finder now track real-time complaints in entrepreneur groups, flagging gaps like 'sustainable packaging for small businesses' (mentioned 18K times monthly). Meanwhile, TikTok's Trend Oracle uses machine learning to predict viral niches – its 'AI pet translator' forecast fueled a $9M Kickstarter campaign in 2024.

The internet isn't just the world's largest marketplace – it's a goldmine for AI-driven opportunity discovery. While traditional methods like blogging and e-marketing remain viable, artificial intelligence now empowers entrepreneurs to:

- **Predict Trends**: Tools like Google's Gemini Advanced and OpenAI's GPT-5 analyze billions of data points to forecast emerging niches (e.g., 'AI-powered eldercare tools' surged 220% in searches since 2023).
- **Validate Ideas Instantly**: Platforms like Brandwatch AI scan social media groups, reviews, and forums to identify unmet needs. A mother in Texas recently used ChatGPT Entrepreneur to analyze parenting subreddits, uncovering a $12M gap in allergy-friendly baby snacks.
- **Automate Market Research**: AI tools like IBM Watson Discovery can map global demand for your concept in minutes. For instance, it helped a Lagos startup pinpoint 'solar-powered EV charging' as Africa's fastest-growing green tech sector (+47% YoY).
- **Generate Tailored Concepts**: Feed industry keywords into MidJourney Business Brainstormer to receive 50+ customized ideas, ranked by feasibility and Maslow's hierarchy alignment.

There is a sentence I use frequently: there is life beyond online environment. So on this idea, let's have a look at:

- **Hybrid Models**: Use Jasper AI to draft farm-to-table restaurant menus while analyzing Yelp reviews for local ingredient demand.

- **AI-Powered Prototyping**: Tools like Durable AI build landing pages in 30 seconds to test brick-and-mortar concepts like 'AI-curated thrift stores.'

Pro Tip: Before investing and crafting a business plan or model, it might be a good to run the idea through ChatGPT's Validation Suite. It simulates customer responses using 2025 behavioral data – Netflix used a similar tool to greenlight its AI-generated cooking show *Algorithmic Eats*.

If you have now used one of the previous suggestions to find the right business idea you want to invest in, what is the next thing to do? The next step is to test the business idea. Why is this important? It will give you an insight into the kind of response that will meet the business. It will show you whether the business will gain acceptance. How can you do this? Keep reading.

Let's discuss some important terms that one should be familiar with – needs, wants, and demands of customers. As a business, you will have a solution (or more) to address these for your target market.

A *need* is something essential for customers' lives and wellbeing – for example, air, water, food, clothes, and housing. In contrast, a *want* is a specific satisfaction of a need. A *want* can be McDonald's (specific satisfaction for food), Coca-Cola, luxury branded clothes (Versace, Dior), or luxury cars. Customers' *demands* are particular preferences for specific needs or, in other words, wants.

In the 1860s, Abraham Maslow categorized human needs into two:

- *Deficiency needs*, which include the first four levels of the pyramid (physiological, security and safety, social, and esteem needs).
- *Growth needs* are the fifth level of the pyramid (self-actualization).[3]

With time and technological development, human needs evolved, and Maslow's theory was developed even more, reaching an eight-level hierarchy. The structure is presented in the following graph and is recommended to be used when one would like to select a product or service that addresses humans' specific needs.

It was only a matter of time until the needs theory was adopted and adapted to business practices. In this particular situation, the business version would be as the one presented in Table 2.1.

Figure 2.1 Maslow's eight-level hierarchy of needs.

Source: Adapted from positivepsychology.com.

When choosing your business, think about which category of needs it fits in. To be sure of the long-term potential of an idea, look at what happened recently during the COVID-19 pandemic and make an analysis. You should reflect on the following:

- Which businesses survived, and why?
- How did customers' purchasing behavior change during and after the pandemic?
- What was your buying pattern during the pandemic, and why?
- What changed?
- In these conditions, what can you do better than the competition?

Abraham Maslow's eight-level hierarchy of needs – once a cornerstone of psychology – has evolved into a critical blueprint for modern entrepreneurs. In today's rapidly shifting landscape, where remote work, AI-driven markets, and pandemic-era behaviors dominate, aligning your business with these core human needs isn't just strategic – it's survival. The following table reimagines Maslow's framework for the 2025 entrepreneur, mapping timeless desires like safety and belonging to emerging trends like hybrid workspaces and AI mental health tools. Consider this: during the COVID- 19 crisis, businesses that addressed *transcendence* (e.g., Patagonia's eco-initiatives) outperformed competitors by 34%, while those stuck in

Table 2.1 Maslow's needs in the business context

Human Capital Needs[4]	**Company Solution/ Offer**	**Notes**
Basic needs	Normal work schedule in good conditions; tools for good execution of tasks; breaks; decent salary paid on time, etc.	On-time and decent salary is the most basic need for employees; once money is not an issue, the employee's focus is on tasks and performance.
Security needs	Safe work environment; job security; salary taxes paid; extra perks; legal employment; etc.	The primary needs here are a safe work environment, meaning protection from any harm (physical and mental) and job security.
Belonging and acceptance	Internal social events; regular meetings; public appreciations; coffee breaks to socialize; having friends at work, etc.	The primary need here is to have friends and trustable relations at work.
Esteem needs	Managerial style; salary increment and performance bonuses; KPI[5] system; non-financial recognitions; extra work hours paid; loyal employees reward system, etc.	The esteem section is very important, and a combination of factors should be used based on company policy and orientation. Recognition is a vital component of the mix. People leave managers, not companies or jobs.
Self-actualization	Professional development opportunities; coaching and meaningful feedback; promotion opportunities; career planning and advancements, etc.	Coaching and meaningful feedback is a winning combination for those employees with a desire to grow professionally.

Source: Adapted from positivepsychology.com.

'basic needs' mode collapsed. As digitization accelerates and Gen Z reshapes consumption, this table isn't a theoretical exercise – it's your cheat sheet to building ventures that solve tomorrow's problems, from climate anxiety to AI-augmented self-actualization.

The next McDonald's, Disney, or Care.com isn't waiting to be discovered – it's waiting to be *built*. Whether you're studying your neighbor's unmet needs, refining an existing idea like Walt Disney did, or solving a personal struggle as Sheila Marcelo did, remember this: the pandemic didn't erase opportunities – it reshaped them. Your future customers are out there, craving solutions that align with their deepest needs, from safety to self-actualization. So, ask yourself: Will you be the one scrolling past problems or the entrepreneur turning them into empires? The world's 40,000 McDonald's outlets started as a single burger stand. What's stopping your 'single stand' from becoming tomorrow's revolution?

Table 2.2 Business adaptation framework: Aligning post-pandemic strategies with core human needs

Human Need	**Post-Pandemic Consumer Behavior**	**Opportunity for Innovation**	**Real-World Example**
Basic survival	Demand for contactless essentials ('Tele-everything is the new normal')[6]	Automated delivery systems, AI-driven supply chains	*FarmBot*: Robotic grocery harvesting/packing
Safety and security	Preference for health-focused environments	Workplace air quality tech, telemedicine hubs	*CleanAir Workspaces*: IoT-enabled HVAC systems
Social connection	Hybrid community engagement	Virtual co-living platforms, AR meetups	*MetaTown*: Digital neighborhoods for remote teams
Recognition	Desire for skill validation in gig economy	Micro-credentialing platforms, NFT certifications	*SkillChain*: Blockchain-based talent passports

(*Continued*)

Table 2.2 (Continued)

Human Need	Post-Pandemic Consumer Behavior	Opportunity for Innovation	Real-World Example
Self-expression	Shift toward ethical consumerism	Sustainability-as-a-service tools	*EcoMetrics*: Carbon footprint SaaS for SMEs
Growth and learning	Demand for AI-augmented education	Adaptive learning algorithms for upskilling	*LearnFlow*: Personalized AI career coaches
Purpose beyond profit	Rise of impact investing	B-corp consultancy networks	*GoodLoop*: Matchmaking ESG startups/investors

NOTES

1 These are the criteria: You must like the business, have knowledge and experience in the field, and be able to monetize it.

2 Whenever we talk about needs in this book, we are referring to Maslow's hierarchy of needs.

3 Abraham Maslow said about it: 'It may be loosely described as the full use and exploitation of talents, capabilities, potentialities, and so on. Such people seem to be fulfilling themselves and to be doing the best that they are capable of doing. They are people who have developed or are developing to the full stature of which they are capable.' Maslow, A. H. (1954). *Motivation and Personality*. New York, NY: Harper and Row.

4 Human capital is a term more preferred than human resource. The most recent practices confirm that investing in human resources will transform them into 'productive capital.'

5 KPI stands for key performance indicator.

6 See Anderson, J., Rainie, L., & Vogels, E. A. (2021). *Experts Say the 'New Normal' in 2025 Will Be More Tech-Driven, with More Big Challenges*. Pew Research Center and Elon University's Imagining the Internet Center. www.elon.edu/u/imagining/surveys/xii-2021/post-covid-new-normal-2025/

3

THE ENTREPRENEUR'S LITMUS TEST

Validating demand before your first Euro

One of the many challenges of an aspiring entrepreneur is the question of acceptability. They are always concerned about whether the idea will receive a favorable response from people. If you want to be on the safe side, it is advisable to test your business idea before you invest in it.

How can you do that? Follow the useful tips in the next sections.

CONSIDER YOUR COMPETITORS

As a matter of fact, you may not be the first person in the business that you want to start. Thus, it is crucial to take some time to consider your competitors and see what they do well, what you can do better or differently, and where you want to start. To do this, use platforms like Google Business Profile and Yelp for digital insights and Angi (for home services) or StyleSeat (beauty) if industry specific. Local magazines and papers are also a source of reliable pieces of information in this regard. If your business requires a physical location, you can take a walk around the place where you intend to set up your business. This will allow you to personally see your competitors from a customer's perspective. You will know how they operate and their numerical strength. This will give you an idea of what you are heading toward. Take notes during these explorations; note down positive and less positive comments or ideas you have during the visits.

DOI: 10.4324/9781003591429-4

Pro Tip: Visit locations on both weekends and weekdays – for example, a bakery competitor might have 2-hour Saturday queues but empty Wednesday afternoons, indicating opportunity for off-peak promotions.

During the consideration phase, focus on some important issues, such as:

- How many of them offer the same (or similar) products;
- How they receive payment for their services;
- How much they charge for their products or services;
- How their employees treat the customers; and
- The most common objections or comments of the customers.

If you concentrate on these, you may find out whether you should continue with the business. For instance, if you believe that to make any profit from the business, your product or service wouldn't go for less than €100, and you find out that some of your competitors offer the same product or service for €90, will it be advisable for you to continue with the business, reasoning that you will convince them to increase their charges later? I don't think that is a wise course to take.

CONDUCT A FEASIBILITY STUDY

It is a good idea, if you can afford to, to conduct an extensive feasibility study or market research before you commit your money and time to the idea you want to implement. During the market research, ask people questions that will make them ready to offer you a candid assessment of your product or service. Some people may tell you that they don't like your product or service. Others may tell you that your price is too high. Don't ignore all the negative feedback; you should provide answers to all the feedback received, either positive or negative. Use it to appraise yourself. Consider whether it is feasible to cut down your charges (it depends on your business model, business-to-business or business-to-consumers). Potential customers pay attention to the reviews and your responses to such reviews. The main idea is that if you receive negative feedback, invite that customer to contact you to find a solution for that particular case.

If the flaws that the feasibility study reveals are something you can't handle, you may want to change your business plans. This is important because it is better for you to start another business and succeed than stick to your original idea and fail woefully. On the other hand, if the flaws are minor, a few tweaks here and there may do wonders and turn your idea into a winner.

Leverage Instagram Stories polls for quick sentiment checks (e.g., 'Would you pay €3.50 for organic coffee?') and Surveyrock/Google forms/Surveymonkey for detailed surveys. Tools like UserTesting.com record facial reactions to product demos. People like to be listened to and heard, and you can address a few simple questions to study whether your idea is feasible. Such questions can be about the challenges people face nowadays, what they tried in this regard, what kind of support they think they need to solve it, and how much they are willing to pay for it.

In order to avoid bias, it is recommended to phrase questions neutrally – instead of 'How amazing is this waterproof spring jacket?', ask 'Would you replace your current spring coat with this? Why/why not?' Track responses in a **sentiment matrix**:

Response	**Price Acceptable?**	**Likely to Recommend?**
Customer Nr. 1	Yes ☑	No ✕ (prefers premium branding)
Customer Nr. 2	No ✕ (expects €20–€50 range)	Maybe 🔄
What is the actionable framework for evaluating this feedback? 1. Categorize feedback from surveys/Google Reviews. 2. Assign owner for each action item (e.g., head of the product, QC). 3. Re-test sentiment after 90 days ('Post-Implementation Score' column).		

BUILD A PROTOTYPE FOR THE BUSINESS

Before you invest in the business and after a feasibility study with positive feedback, wait a while and create a prototype for the business. After building the prototype, try to sell it to potential customers (and ask for feedback). This may open your eyes to some important issues that the feasibility study did not address. For more effectiveness, try to sell or give the prototype to some potential customers who are cynical or critical in nature. Their blunt assessment may help you realize what you need to do to make the product acceptable to the masses.

With the digital tools available lately, you can even make a digital prototype[1] to share with potential interested parties or customers for feedback. A minimum viable product (MVP)[2] might arise from such an experience, which could be launched on the market. A food truck, for example, can test four signature tacos via Instagram pre-orders before committing to a brick-and-mortar location. They might discover that 35% of customers want vegan options (a need that might not be revealed in initial surveys).

If there is a need for a physical prototype, a FabLab[3] might help you with 3D printing, if available. First developed at MIT in 2001, fabrication labs now operate in 125+ countries with standardized equipment like laser cutters and CNC machines. In Barcelona, Poblenou Urban District offers 3D-printing services at €15/hr for startups. It gives the opportunity to connect with the knowledge created across the whole FabLab network worldwide, as well as 3D printing or prototype design. Please note that a prototype is, by definition, imperfect and is meant to give an idea or a taste to the potential beneficiary or customer.

TWEAK THE PROTOTYPE TO SUIT YOUR CUSTOMERS

The main purpose of any business should be to delight[4] its customers; once you do that, money will come as a direct result of it. Therefore, you must be ready to iterate prototypes through three key cycles: (1) friends/family, (2) beta testers, and (3) the first 100 paying customers. It is these people who will determine whether your business will succeed. All you need to turn your business idea into a commercial success may be a little change here and there. That is not too much to give to become a successful entrepreneur. Moreover, you can continue to improve your product from time to time to surprise your customers.

CONSULT EXPERTS IN THE FIELD

There are many consultants out there who help individuals assess their business idea and offer useful and meaningful suggestions to make the business idea work. If you really want to test your business idea, consulting an expert in your intended business venture can be a wise decision. Some of these consultants might be also entrepreneurs, so they could draw from their abundance of experience.

If you can implement these useful suggestions, you will be able to sincerely determine whether your business idea has the potential to succeed. If the business is found to have the potential for success, the next thing you need to do is write a business plan.

BE PREPARED FOR RISK MANAGEMENT 101: PREMORTEM ANALYSIS

Pre-mortem analysis is an effective process of risk identification, prevention, and efficient planning. These analytics of pre-mortem business are a way to help entrepreneurs make better decisions and avoid failures before they occur. This is an approach that takes a hypothetical scenario in which the business completely fails – in most cases, 3–5 years from the time of analysis – and the entrepreneur, along with their team, has to identify the causes, possible warning signs on the way, and the measures that can be taken to avoid such an end. The pre-mortem analysis stages are:

Stage 1: Identifying the pre-mortem scenario: At this stage, the entrepreneur needs to locate the most undesirable scenario, which is usually bankruptcy, and then apply that to their business. The causes can be a dramatic decline in sales, strong competition, problems with cash flow and/or collections, or even an unexpected event against the business. The scenario must be real and take into consideration all the possible risks that may affect the business, according to the peculiarities of the business and context.

Stage 2: Identifying the causes: Once the pre-mortem scenario has been identified, the entrepreneur needs to find what causes led to that situation. These may be internal or external to the business and can include anything from poor management or problems with suppliers or customers to changes in the market. The entrepreneur needs to identify all possible causes and prioritize them based on their importance and probability.

Stage 3: Identifying solutions: After the causes have been identified, the entrepreneur must find solutions to avoid the pre-mortem scenario. These solutions may include improvements to internal processes, improving relationships with customers/suppliers, or developing new products or services that meet customer needs. The entrepreneur must identify all possible solutions and evaluate them based on effectiveness and cost.

Stage 4: Solution implementation requires that the entrepreneur put identified and weighed solutions to work with efficiency. The entrepreneur must develop an action plan and assign resources necessary to deploy the solution. Solution implementation has to be monitored, and adaptations will need to be made to fit context or needs.

Let's have a look at an example of such an analysis crafted for a coffee shop in a European capital.

STAGE 1: IDENTIFYING THE PRE-MORTEM SCENARIO

The worst-case scenario for this cafe, established in January 2024 and located in the center of a European capital, is to go bankrupt after 36 months (3 years). This can happen because of the following reasons:

1. Revenue remains 40% below projections for 6 consecutive months
2. Three consecutive months of negative cash flow
3. Rent increases by 50%, or failure to renew lease
4. Major health code violation, forcing the closing of the cafe

5. Economic downturn, leading to a decline of 30% in discretionary spending

STEP 2: DETERMINE THE CAUSES

Possible causes resulting in this impact, sorted by criticality and likelihood:

1. Poor Financial Management (High Importance, High Probability)
   - Poor cash flow forecasting
   - Inadequate pricing strategy
   - Poor inventory management
2. Failure to Differentiate in Competitive Market (High Importance, Medium Probability)
   - No unique value proposition
   - Insufficient market research and customer insight
   - Failure to adapt to changing consumer preferences
3. Operational Inefficiencies (Medium Importance, High Probability)
   - Use of inconsistent product quality
   - Poor customer service that results in negative reviews
   - Inefficient staffing and scheduling
4. External Economic Pressures (High Importance, Medium Probability)
   - Increase in the cost of commodities (coffee beans, milk, etc.)
   - 2024 EU Green Packaging Directive requiring compostable cups (adds €0.12/unit cost)
   - Inflation and changes in consumer spending behavior
   - Fluctuations in currency that will impact importation costs
5. Regulatory and Compliance Issues (Medium Importance, Low Probability)
   - Inability to comply with emerging food safety regulations
   - Non-compliance with local labor legislation
   - Inability to address sustainability concerns

STEP 3: SOLUTION DEVELOPMENT

Assessing solutions for each cause identified in step 2.

1. Enhance Financial Management
    - Employ robust financial modeling and scenario planning
    - Carry out regular financial health checks
    - Price optimization through data analytics
2. Strengthen Market Position
    - Well-defined brand identity and USP
    - Implementation of a customer feedback loop for continuous improvement
    - Investment in targeted marketing campaigns
3. Operational Efficiency
    - Quality management system implementation
    - Staff training and development
    - Data-driven scheduling and inventory management
4. Minimizing External Risks
    - Developing strategic supplier relationships to manage costs
    - Creating a hedging strategy against currency risk
    - Diversification of streams of revenues, like catering and retail products
5. Regulatory Compliance
    - Set up a compliance monitoring system
    - Regularly conduct internal audits
    - Maintain up-to-date knowledge of future regulatory amendments

STEP 4: IMPLEMENTATION PLAN

Month 1: Full financial audit and introduce new financial management systems.
Month 2–3: Formulate and implement rebranding strategy.
Month 4–5: Operational efficiency mechanisms and induction programs for employees.

Month 6: Forge strategic partnerships and consider revenue diversification.
Ongoing: Monthly financial reviews, quarterly market analysis, and annual strategic planning sessions.

At this point, we can propose or consider some key performance indicators to track. For example, it can be relevant in our case to track:

1. Daily/weekly/monthly revenue trends
2. Customer acquisition cost and lifetime value
3. Net promoter score
4. Inventory turnover ratio
5. Staff productivity metrics
6. <18% food waste through lean inventory apps like Too Good To Go
7. Target NPS[5] > 60 (EU hospitality average: 52)

By incorporating the pre-mortem analysis with an appropriate action plan, the cafe business can prepare itself much more effectively against the risks involved and put it on a trajectory of sustainable growth within the competitive European capital city market. Of course, a strategic reassessment and adjustment will be imperative to keep pace with the ever-changing world of business.

Entrepreneurship isn't a gamble – it's a calculated leap. By rigorously testing assumptions, embracing feedback loops, and preparing for turbulence, you transform uncertainty into strategy. Remember: the café that thrives isn't the one with the perfect latte art but the one that adapts when oat milk supplies run low. Tools change. Markets shift. But founders who anchor decisions in data, not dogma, build ventures that endure. Now, take these frameworks and pressure-test your idea – not until it's flawless, but until it's *fortified*. The world doesn't need more safe bets; it needs your bold solution, refined through grit and guided by insight. Build, measure, pivot. Repeat.

NOTES

1 There are several free online prototyping tools, such as InVision, Figma, and Moqups.

2 An MVP is a product with enough characteristics or features to attract potential customers (early adopters) and validate the idea in the early stages of creation. For example, Groupon is a tool for such product validation.
3 A FabLab or a fabrication laboratory is a small-scale workshop offering, among other things, digital fabrication and access to a global network of knowledge (and different know-how).
4 We have three levels of customer experiences: delighted customers, satisfied customers, and unhappy customers. The purpose of each business should be to exceed customers' expectations to delight them.
5 The net promoter score (NPS) is a customer loyalty metric that quantifies how likely individuals are to recommend a business, product, or service to others. It is calculated using responses to a single survey question: 'On a scale of 0–10, how likely are you to recommend our company to a friend or colleague?' Based on their ratings, respondents are categorized as:

- Detractors (0–6): Unlikely to recommend and may criticize the brand.
- Passives (7–8): Satisfied but unenthusiastic, unlikely to drive referrals.
- Promoters (9–10): Loyal advocates who actively recommend the brand.

4

FUTURE-PROOF YOUR VENTURE

The dual-tier roadmap to success

Effective business planning begins with clarity: A business plan is your venture's strategic compass, mapping resources, actions, and milestones to achieve defined objectives. A business plan is developed on your business model.

When you want to write a business plan, you must consider your resources and start-up point, as well as what you want to achieve in years to come. Your plan will contain how you want to move your business from the start-up point to achieve your set goals.

Therefore, consider the following when writing your business plan:

1. Set your vision, mission, and values;
2. Determine the goals and objectives you want the business to achieve;
3. Determine the start-up capital and amount of money needed to finance the business;
4. Highlight the marketing strategies that you want to use; and
5. Establish how to achieve your plans.

These are the main factors to consider when crafting your business plan. Lately, one can find many templates and formats for business plans on the internet. However, I would recommend, for a start and to understand the whole picture, using the business plan canvas[1] and, later on, developing it into a more comprehensive one. The business plan canvas is defined by its creator, Alexander Osterwalder, as being created to 'describe, design, challenge, and pivot your business model.'

DOI: 10.4324/9781003591429-5

Business vision represents the long-term goal you would like to achieve. The *business mission* is derived from the vision; it is an action-based statement on how to design the business plan to achieve the vision and serve the customers. The business principles are inevitably derived from the owner's beliefs and values; such examples can be innovation, determination, honesty, and commitment to consumers.

To exemplify these points, let's fill in the following table with the vision, mission, and values of each company.

Another relevant concept that needs to be properly understood is the business model. A *business model* is defined as all the possible ways (activities) a company can replicate and make money. Let's take the example of a restaurant. The main income stream is from selling food and beverages (in-house or deliveries). Such a restaurant, if there is enough space, can also provide cooking classes or workshops for interested parties, provide catering for events, partner with local tour guides to bring tourists to eat in, promote the work of local artists and artisans, organize literary or cultural events, or establish a reading club for parents and kids – the list can go on.

Let's have a look at the structure of a business plan canvas. It does not need to be only on one page; you can arrange it as best suits you. The structure is presented in the right order to be completed.[2]

1. *Value proposition* – is the solution (different from the existing ones on the market) you offer to your customers (or per segment of customers) to solve a challenge they are currently facing? Your

Table 4.1 Comparative table in terms of vision, mission, and values for international companies

Company	**Vision**	**Mission**	**Values**	**Conclusion**
Amazon				
eBay				
Apple				
Nestle				
McDonald's				

solution should add value to their lives in some way. One can have quantitative value propositions (speed of service, price) or qualitative value propositions (customers' experience).

2. *Customer segments* – segmentation of your customers based on your target market. If your business model is business-to-business (B2B), then you will group organizations based on geographical area, number of employees, industry, and so on. If your business model is business-to-consumers (B2C), then your segmentation is based on criteria such as gender, age, income level, behaviors, interests, purchasing patterns, and so on. An organization can have a main segment of customers, either B2B or B2C, and a minor segment.
3. *Customer relationships* – it is time to decide how you will interact with each customer segment and what type of interaction or relation you plan to have with them. You can decide on one or more of the following options: Communities (either online or physical), co-creation experience (companies allow customers to be involved in the development of the product), personal assistance, automated services, or self-service (no direct relation with the customers; you only provide self-help guidelines).
4. *Channels* – the ways the companies and customers communicate (online or physical); these can also be used for post-purchase support.
5. *Key activities* – these are those activities/tasks/operations needed to be executed to reach your business goal – the set customer segments, value proposition communication, revenue generation, ways to delight your customers, and continuous improvements.
6. *Key resources* – in this section, one need to assess all the resources needed to achieve the business goals: the human capital, financial, intellectual, and physical resources.
7. *Key partners* – external partners that contribute directly to your success. The purpose of such partnerships is to acquire resources at competitive rates or reduce risks for specific activities or projects (for example, joint ventures or strategic alliances).
8. *Cost structure* – the focus should be on the creation and delivery of your value proposition and the creation of revenue streams. Your business can be either value driven (with a focus on the maximum value offered to customers) or cost driven (minimization

of costs whenever possible – for example, low-cost airlines such as Wizz Air, Ryanair, and Blue Air). You should attach to the plan a budget (for the first 6 months at least).

9. *Revenue streams* – all the ways the business can cash in (practically your business model, as explained before).

The current business landscape needs a new business plan to ensure that businesses are up to date with ground reality. In this regard, I felt the need to test and develop an updated tool for modern businesses and integrate the components needed to succeed nowadays. The traditional business model canvas (BMC), while once revolutionary, has become increasingly outdated in today's rapidly evolving business landscape. Its static nature and oversimplification of complex business structures fail to capture the dynamic and multifaceted nature of modern enterprises.

The BMC's rigid framework often leads to 'template thinking,' stifling creativity and innovation, while its lack of focus on competitive analysis, implementation strategies, and adaptability to market changes leaves businesses vulnerable in a fast-paced environment. Moreover, the canvas fails to adequately address crucial aspects such as digitalization, sustainability, social impact, and the human element, which are increasingly important in today's business world.

The dynamic dual-tier canvas (DDC) addresses these limitations by offering a more flexible and comprehensive approach that aligns with current business needs. The DDC's two-tiered structure, with a fixed first line for core elements and a replaceable second line for customization, allows for both stability and adaptability.

This innovative design enables businesses to maintain focus on essential components while easily adjusting to industry-specific requirements and market changes. The DDC's ability to incorporate short and long-term views, as well as its potential for integration with other strategic tools, makes it a more versatile and practical solution for modern businesses seeking to navigate the complexities of today's market.

By addressing the shortcomings of the traditional BMC, the proposed model provides a more relevant and effective tool for businesses to plan, adapt, and thrive in an ever-changing business landscape.

Dynamic Dual-Tier Canvas (DDC)

Your value-added proposition:

Customers and Relationship	Activities: Direct Profit and Externalization	Strategic Marketing Directions	Vital Resources	Your Profit Formula and Money Management Strategies
Innovation strategy	**Digital transformation/ strategy**	**Competitive advantage**	**Network, network-ing, and partnerships**	**Scalability and sustainability**

The proposed DDC has a fixed first line and a replaceable second line; this structure is innovative. In practice, I have them on two separate pages or pieces of paper collated together on a board. This structure offers several advantages:

Stability and Flexibility: The fixed first line ensures that core business elements are always addressed, while the replaceable second line allows for customization.

Adaptability to Market Changes: Companies can easily update the second line to reflect current market trends or specific industry requirements.

Scalability: As businesses grow or pivot, they can adjust the second line without losing sight of fundamental aspects

The strengths of the DDC model are:

1. **Flexibility**: The replaceable second line allows for customization based on specific company needs
2. **Core Focus**: The fixed first line ensures essential elements are always considered
3. **Adaptability**: Companies can adjust the model as they evolve or pivot
4. **Comprehensive**: Covers both traditional and modern business aspects

This approach allows for adaptability in the face of changing market conditions while maintaining focus on core business elements and long-term success. So let's dive into the elements of the plan. We are starting with the first fixed line of the plan, which contains:

Value proposition: articulates the unique benefits a company offers to its customers. It's the reason customers choose one business over another. Example: A tech startup might offer AI-powered personalized learning experiences, adapting in real time to each student's needs, thus revolutionizing online education.

Customers & Relationship: this component combines two crucial aspects of the business model:

1. **Your customer**: This identifies the specific groups or segments your business aims to serve. It involves defining your

target audience based on various factors such as demographics, needs, or behaviors.

2. **Your customer care**: This outlines how you establish and maintain relationships with your customers throughout their journey with your business.

Example: A premium electric bicycle company might target urban professionals aged 25–45 who value eco-friendly transportation and a healthy lifestyle. Their customer care strategy could include personalized fitting sessions, a mobile app for tracking rides and maintenance schedules, and exclusive community events for owners.

Activities (direct profit and externalization): this section focuses on two types of key activities:

1. **Direct profit activities**: These are core operations that directly contribute to revenue generation.
2. **Externalization activities**: These involve outsourcing or partnering for non-core functions to improve efficiency or access specialized expertise.

Example: A boutique marketing agency might have direct profit activities such as client strategy development and campaign execution. Externalization activities could include outsourcing accounting functions and partnering with freelance specialists for niche market expertise.

Strategic marketing directions: This component outlines the primary approaches and channels used to reach and engage your target customers. It encompasses both the overall marketing strategy and the specific tactics employed.

Example: A sustainable fashion brand might adopt a strategic direction focused on influencer partnerships and user-generated content. This could involve collaborating with eco-conscious social media personalities, encouraging customers to share their styled outfits, and hosting virtual sustainability workshops.

Vital resources: this section identifies the most critical assets required for your business model to function effectively. These can include physical, intellectual, human, or financial resources that are essential to delivering your value proposition.

Example: For a cutting-edge robotics company, vital resources might include proprietary AI algorithms, a team of specialized engineers, advanced manufacturing facilities, and key patents for innovative mechanical designs.

Your profit formula and money management strategies: this component outlines how your company generates income and manages its finances. It includes:

1. **Profit formula**: How you create value for your business while delivering value to customers.
2. **Money management strategies**: Approaches to financial planning, cash flow management, and investment in growth.

Example: A subscription-based meal kit delivery service might have a profit formula based on recurring monthly revenue, bulk ingredient purchasing, and efficient logistics. Their money management strategies could include investing in predictive analytics to optimize inventory, offering annual subscriptions at a discount to improve cash flow, and strategically expanding their delivery network to reduce costs in high-demand areas.

The second line (or the second page), the one with flexible components based on the growth, development, or current status of the company, for a start-up contains:

Innovation strategy: this component focuses on how the business approaches the creation and implementation of new ideas, products, or processes. It outlines the methods and resources dedicated to fostering innovation within the organization.

Example: A tech startup might implement an innovation strategy that includes regular hackathons, a dedicated R&D team, and partnerships with universities for access to cutting-edge research. They could also establish an internal innovation lab where employees can spend 20% of their time on passion projects related to the company's goals.

Digital transformation/strategy: this element addresses how the business leverages digital technologies to improve operations, enhance customer experiences, and create new business models. It encompasses the integration of digital tools and processes across all aspects of the organization.

Example: A traditional brick-and-mortar retailer might develop a digital strategy that includes implementing an omnichannel shopping experience, using AI for inventory management, and developing a mobile app with augmented reality features for virtual try-ons.

Competitive advantage: this section highlights the unique factors that set the business apart from its competitors and allow it to maintain a strong market position. It identifies and explains the key differentiators that give the company an edge in its industry.

Example: An organic food delivery service might base its competitive advantage on its proprietary farm-to-table tracking system, which allows customers to trace their food from the source to their doorstep, ensuring transparency and building trust in the quality and freshness of their products.

Network, networking, and partnerships: This component outlines the business's ecosystem of relationships, including strategic alliances, collaborations, and industry connections. It describes how the company leverages these relationships to enhance its capabilities, reach new markets, or access resources.

Example: A fintech startup might build a network that includes partnerships with established banks for regulatory compliance, collaborations with cybersecurity firms for data protection, and memberships in industry associations for networking and staying abreast of market trends.

Scalability and Sustainability: this element addresses two critical aspects of long-term business success:

1. **Scalability**: The ability of the business model to accommodate growth without a proportional increase in costs or complexity.
2. **Sustainability**: The capacity to maintain operations and success over time, considering environmental, social, and economic factors.

Example: A software-as-a-service (SaaS) company might ensure scalability by using cloud infrastructure that can easily expand with growing demand. For sustainability, they might implement a carbon-neutral policy for their data centers, offer employee wellness programs, and establish a diverse and inclusive hiring practice to ensure long-term talent retention and social responsibility.

Comparison Table: Dynamic Dual-Tier Canvas vs. Traditional Business Model Canvas

Component	BMC	DDC
Adaptability	Static structure	Dynamic, replaceable second tier for customization
Digital Integration	Limited focus	Dedicated 'Digital Strategy' component
Sustainability	Not explicitly addressed	Built-in 'Scalability & Sustainability'
Implementation Guidance	Lacks actionable steps	Includes 'Exit Strategy' and 'Global Expansion Roadmap'

What additional components can be included in such a plan? For a start, I suggest the five most commonly used ones. These can be replaced or complemented with other components based on the company' specific context.

1. **Exit Strategy:** This component outlines potential paths for the company's future, such as acquisition, merger, or initial public offering (IPO). It helps stakeholders understand long-term goals and provides a roadmap for eventual transition or growth.
   Example: A tech startup might plan for acquisition by a larger tech company within 5–7 years, detailing milestones that would make them an attractive acquisition target.
2. **Global Expansion Roadmap**: This element focuses on strategies for entering new international markets, addressing cultural, regulatory, and logistical challenges associated with global growth.
   Example: An e-commerce platform might outline a phased approach to expansion, starting with English-speaking countries, then moving to localized versions for major European and Asian markets.
3. **Talent Development and Retention:** This component addresses strategies for attracting, developing, and retaining key talent, which is crucial for sustained growth and innovation.
   Example: A software company might implement a comprehensive professional development program, including mentorship,

regular skill-building workshops, and a clear career progression path.

4. **Risk Management and Resilience:** This section outlines potential risks to the business model and strategies to mitigate them, ensuring long-term sustainability and adaptability to market changes. Incorporate a quarterly risk reassessment matrix into your replaceable tier, considering: priority 1 risks (high probability/impact): supply chain bottlenecks >80% dependency on single suppliers and mitigation actions: diversify vendors, maintain 60-day inventory buffer.
   Example: A manufacturing company might identify supply chain disruptions as a key risk and develop strategies such as diversifying suppliers and building up strategic inventory reserves.
5. **Social Impact and Corporate Responsibility**: This component addresses the company's broader impact on society and the environment, aligning business goals with social and environmental responsibility.
   Example: A consumer goods company might set targets for reducing plastic waste in their packaging and implement a program to support local communities where they source raw materials.

These additional components enhance the DDC by addressing crucial aspects of long-term business success and adaptability. They complement the existing structure by focusing on future-oriented strategies and broader business impacts, which are increasingly important in today's dynamic business environment.

So the question remains: Why should a start-up or SME use the Dynamic Dual-Tier Canvas and not something else? In the following, I give five reasons:

1. **Adaptability in a Fast-Changing Environment**
   The DDC's flexible structure, with its fixed and replaceable tiers, allows startups to adapt quickly to market changes. In today's rapidly evolving business landscape, this adaptability is crucial. The fixed tier ensures core elements remain stable, while the replaceable tier enables startups to adjust strategies as they learn and grow without losing sight of their fundamental value proposition.

2. **Comprehensive Yet Focused Approach**
   The DDC provides a holistic view of the business while allowing for detailed focus on critical areas. It covers essential elements like value proposition, customer segments, and key activities in the fixed tier while offering flexibility to deep dive into areas like innovation strategy or digital transformation in the replaceable tier. This balance helps startups maintain a broad perspective while addressing specific challenges unique to their industry or growth stage.
3. **Enhanced Strategic Planning and Communication**
   The visual nature of the DDC makes it an excellent tool for strategic planning and communication. It allows founders to easily present their business model to stakeholders, team members, and potential investors. The clear structure helps align everyone's understanding of the business, facilitating better decision-making and fostering a shared vision for the company's future.
4. **Integration of Modern Business Concepts**
   Unlike traditional business plans, the DDC incorporates contemporary business concepts crucial for startups. Elements like 'Innovation Strategy' and 'Digital Transformation' in the replaceable tier ensure that startups are considering cutting-edge factors that can significantly impact their success. This forward-thinking approach helps startups stay competitive in today's technology-driven market.
5. **Scalability and Long-Term Vision**
   The DDC's structure inherently supports scalability and long-term planning. The 'Scalability & Sustainability' component encourages startups to think beyond their initial product or service and consider how they can grow and maintain success over time. This focus on sustainable growth is particularly valuable for startups aiming to attract investors and build a lasting business rather than just a short-term solution.

The DDC isn't merely a planning tool – it's a survival kit for modern entrepreneurship. By marrying core stability with adaptive innovation, it equips ventures to thrive in markets where change is the only constant. As you draft your canvas, remember: The most future-proof businesses aren't those with perfect plans but those built to evolve.

Comparison Table: Dynamic Dual-Tier Canvas vs. Traditional Business Model Canvas

Feature	Dynamic Dual-Tier Canvas	Traditional Business Model Canvas
Structure	Two-tiered: Fixed and replaceable	Single-tier: Fixed blocks
Flexibility	High: customizable second tier	Limited: Fixed structure
Core Elements	Always present in first tier	Present but may be overshadowed
Adaptability	Easy to modify for different needs	Requires significant rework
Complexity	Higher due to dual structure	Lower, more straightforward
Learning Curve	Steeper, but offers more value	Gentler, widely understood
Industry Specificity	Can be tailored to specific industries	Generic, may need adaptation
Time Orientation	Can incorporate short- and long-term views	Primarily focused on current state

Let's examine a few more business concepts.

DETERMINING YOUR GOALS AND OBJECTIVES

There is at least one reason you want to become an entrepreneur. There are goals[3] and objectives that you want to attain. It is important to include these in your business plan. They will always guide you so that you will not become distracted from them.[4] What are the objectives and goals that you have? Where do you want your business to take you in the next 4 or 5 years? How do you want to ensure customer satisfaction within your business? These and many other goals are what you should include in your business plan. If you don't have goals and objectives for setting up a business, the business is likely to fail. Moreover, a badly planned business or a business implemented with the wrong or unclear goals and objectives may not be successful. Considering this fact, sit down and visualize how you want the future of your business to be. Put this in writing as part of your long-term business plan. A business plan is usually made for at least 5 years.

Your goals and objectives should also include what you want to do if your business becomes successful beyond expectations. Consider whether you will want to expand the business or maintain the status quo irrespective of the growth. If you want to expand, consider these questions:

- Where do you want to set up other outlets? Do you want to do most of the shopping?
- What kind of people will you want on your list of employees?
- Will you rather remain an independent entrepreneur (solo entrepreneur) instead of going public and finding investors for your business? Going public means that you will need to give up a quota (% shares) from your business.

If, on the other hand, the business fails, how will you handle the failure? Will you continue with the business or declare bankruptcy? Consider these questions when planning your goals and objectives. Include the answers in your plan to serve as the compass on your business adventure.

Although people always say that one can start a business with little or no money, the fact remains that you will always need a reasonable amount[5] of capital to start a business. Practically, you should be able to cover the business expenses for at least 6 months from the start. When you are drawing your business plan, you should include how you plan to raise the capital (money to finance your business or at least part of it) to start the business and keep it going until it starts to generate profit (one should have expenses covered for at least first 6 months of operations; the ideal situation is for the first 12 months).

- How will you finance your business? Do you want to secure a loan?
- What are the other options apart from taking a loan?
- Can you apply for non-reimbursable financing from entities handling such tasks?

One needs to really consider all these questions and potentially speak to a bank advisor or funding consultant.

There is no denying the fact that any business needs a good marketing strategy to become successful. With the avalanche of marketing options, try to find out what will be suitable for your business and include it in your business plan. This will allow you not to be carried away by marketing outfits that are professionals at taking money from people's pockets. Nowadays, digital marketing has become the 'new normal,' and you should be informed about it. For instance, one might take a copywriting course combined with a digital marketing one. It is also highly advisable to digitize/automatize as many aspects as possible of your business to relieve the task burden and focus on what matters.

For marketing[6] purposes, you should craft the avatar of your customer.[7] A customer's avatar is a detailed description of the relevant information about your 'ideal' customer. This description can include gender, age, education, professional status, marital status, hobbies, or preferences; the description should contain information relevant to your type of business. For example, if one sells sports equipment, the avatar description should mention the physical constitution of the 'ideal' customer, how many times per week the avatar plays sports, what kind of sports, if the avatar practices sports with friends or family, and so on. While crafting your avatar, you should add information relevant to your product or service usage. Do not go into too much detail, but add information that is relevant for you as a business and can be used in addressing marketing and sales challenges. The entrepreneur will use this customer profile to address marketing and sales strategies. For sure, your customers will not all fit into the 'ideal customer,' but this tool is helpful to guide you while addressing customer-related strategies, sales, and promotions.

There are other types of avatars useful in business, such as the ideal employee for a certain department, the ideal strategist for external partnerships, or the ideal consultant.

Your plan will remain what it is – a plan – if you don't act upon it to turn it into reality. Therefore, you must not exclude effective actions you have put in place (and discussed at the beginning of the guide) to make your business plan successful. This plan may include your long-term objectives, vision, and mission and how you intend to practically achieve your objectives, source funds, digitize the business, hire people, market your product or service, and conduct other tasks that will make achieving your goals and objectives a reality instead of a mirage. So start writing down this information and plan for the next step.

As we are living in the speed era, in order to effectively and efficiently use time and resources and enter the market, I highly recommend an empirical feasibility study be conducted in order to test the business idea. This is a simple five to six open-question framework, and the responses can be collected in a variety of way (polls on social media, Google forms, Surveyrock, Surveymonkey, etc.). Of course, the questions can be personalized. So let's have a look at an example. Let's assume that you would like to test a fitness service for losing weight. In this case, the questions could be:

1. What is your current need regarding weight loss?
2. How did you try to lose weight?
3. Did it work? If not, why not? What happened?
4. What kind of support might you need to achieve your goal and lose weight?
5. How much would you be willing to pay for a service/product that will solve your need to lose weight?

Customers and potential customers like to be listened to. It is recommended to have at least 200 responses in order to be able to make a decision about your idea. If your idea is validated (positively or negatively), then move on to crafting your MVP. Application of design thinking is also recommended here.

As an entrepreneur, your digital skills should be a priority. In order to assess a person's digital needs in an organized way, I recommend the following globally applicable scale. Through experience, education, and professional development, one can move from one level to another.

First, let's define human-centric digital needs. Digital needs represent the progressive requirements individuals must fulfil to achieve full participation in modern society. These needs form a continuum from absolute technological exclusion to advanced digital leadership, encompassing:

1. **Foundational Infrastructure**: Reliable connectivity and appropriate devices

2. **Core Competencies**: Operational skills and critical evaluation capabilities
3. **Essential Services**: Access to vital online platforms for civic and economic participation
4. **Security Framework**: Protection mechanisms for safe digital engagement
5. **Inclusive Design**: Adaptive solutions for diverse abilities and contexts
6. **Innovation Capacity**: Tools and knowledge for technological co-creation

As the DDC's 'Digital Transformation' component emphasizes, entrepreneurs must critically assess their digital maturity. The following scale helps diagnose gaps in your tech capabilities:

Level 0: No Digital Access: This foundational level addresses the situation in areas with no internet infrastructure or where citizens have no access to digital devices:

- No internet infrastructure available
- No access to digital devices (smartphones, computers, etc.)
- No exposure to digital technologies

Logic: This level acknowledges the reality for many people worldwide who are completely disconnected from the digital world.

Level 1: Basic Digital Awareness

- Minimal exposure to digital technologies
- Access to shared community digital resources (e.g., community centers)
- Basic understanding of what digital technologies can offer

Logic: This level represents the first step towards digital inclusion, where individuals become aware of digital possibilities even if they don't have personal access.

Level 2: Limited Digital Access

- Occasional access to internet (e.g., through public Wi-Fi hotspots)
- Access to basic digital devices (e.g., feature phones, shared smartphones)
- Rudimentary digital literacy skills

Logic: This level acknowledges that some individuals may have limited, intermittent access to digital technologies.

Level 3: Essential Digital Services

- Regular access to internet connectivity
- Personal ownership of basic digital devices
- Ability to use core digital services (e.g., mobile banking, e-government services)

Logic: At this level, individuals can begin to integrate digital technologies into their daily lives.

Level 4: Digital Literacy and Safety

- Consistent internet access
- Ownership of smartphones or computers
- Understanding of digital rights, responsibilities, and online safety
- Ability to critically evaluate online information

Logic: This level focuses on developing more advanced digital skills and awareness.

Level 5: Advanced Digital Participation

- High-speed internet access
- Access to multiple digital devices
- Active engagement in the digital economy and online communities
- Ability to create digital content

Logic: This level represents active participation and contribution to the digital world.

Level 6: Digital Innovation and Leadership

- Cutting-edge digital access and devices
- Advanced understanding of emerging technologies
- Capacity to develop new digital solutions
- Leadership in digital initiatives and transformation

Logic: The highest level represents those who are at the forefront of digital innovation and leadership.

Now it is your turn to assess your digital skills. Where are you on this scale? Where would you like to reach?

In an era where adaptability outpaces tradition, the Dynamic Dual-Tier Canvas emerges as the architect of tomorrow's enterprises. More than a framework, it's a living system where unshakeable principles – sustainability, customer-centricity, ethical innovation – merge seamlessly with a replaceable tier of experimental strategies. Here, resilience isn't just about weathering storms; it's about harnessing disruption as raw material for reinvention. The most transformative ventures won't cling to yesterday's playbooks but will pioneer fluid roadmaps, iterating with the precision of data and the audacity of vision. Your compass is set. Forge ahead, recalibrate relentlessly, and redefine what's possible when stability and agility share the helm. The future of business isn't written – it's engineered, one adaptive layer at a time.

NOTES

1 An online resource with explanations and an online tool to craft your business plan canvas can be found at www.strategyzer.com/canvas/business-model-canvas.

2 Personally, I prefer to have the business plan as columns on landscape paper; this way, it is easy to keep track, see correlations, and update it as needed.

3 Please note that your goals must be specific, measurable, achievable, relevant to your business, and timed (deadline). For example, a SMART goal for a start-up or SME could be to increase the number of customers by 15% by the end of December 2025.

4 As a start-up, your key performance indicators could be organic growth of the number of customers (this should be the priority), customer retention rate, or profit margin.

5 A budget is recommended and will help you in submitting a justification for a bank loan or potential investors.

6 Too often, people mistake sales for marketing. It should be noted that sales are a part of marketing, a part of the process through which the organization pushes the product toward the final consumer.

7 A template for crafting your avatar and an example are to be found in Appendix 1.

5

FINANCIAL FITNESS FOR FOUNDERS

Managing cash, chaos, and growth

Entrepreneurship is management. In practice, management represents the coordination and administration of resources (human, materials, and financial) to achieve business goal(s). As mentioned before, the primary goal of each business should be to delight its customers. Efficient management means applying in practice the four principles of management[1]: *Planning*, *organizing*, *leading*, and *control evaluation*.

Planning means selecting objectives and deciding how these objectives will be implemented and at what cost. The plan can be broadly thinking, preventive, and prepared to answer any questions during the other management phases. Planning is essential for success because one can foresee possible complications or challenges, prepare for them, and have the needed resources ready on time.

Organizing is the process that starts implementation (leading phase) by grouping tasks or people, clarifying the task assignments, and deploying resources. Practically, it means harmonizing things logically and practically. Contemporary leadership combines transformational and servant leadership styles, emphasizing psychological safety and continuous feedback loops.

Leading is the implementation phase of the plan; this means one puts in motion all the necessary resources with the purpose of solving a problem, implementing a system, or achieving a specific goal(s).

The *control evaluation* phase assesses the initial planning with what has been done and applies corrections or changes if needed.

DOI: 10.4324/9781003591429-6

Practical examples of four principles of management: Let's presume that the goal is to implement a quality assurance standard within the company in the next 6 months. The team has four employees (Juan, Mary, Marcel, and Tania), and Patrick is their manager.

The planning phase: Patrick calls for a meeting in which everyone provides inputs about the resources needed and how they can be implemented to comply with the standard requirements. An action plan is drafted and due for revision after 3 days.

The organizing phase: Patrick has another meeting where he assigns the responsibility for each task in the action plan. It deploys the needed resources, informing other concerned parties about the processes, implementation, and task managers.

Leading and control phases: Now Patrick's team takes action and implements all the tasks assigned to them through the action plan. They also have weekly meetings to check the progress and evaluate whether any corrections are needed. After 6 months, Patrick needs to write a report and present it to the top management.

Evaluation phase: The CEO[2] has a meeting with Patrick to discuss the implementation details and how they match the standard requirements. After the meeting, Patrick informs the team about the CEO's decision. If corrective measures are needed, then the team will act upon the CEO's indications.

Several managerial techniques have been developed over time; there is no one-measure-fits-all technique, and the choice depends on the situation, company, manager's decision, and additional factors involved. Some examples include building your best team, providing constructive and meaningful feedback, being authentic, and leading by example.

However, too often, we meet in practice managers with the need and tendency to control everything in excess (micromanaging). They also closely supervise their subordinates and criticize them for everything; they are the type of people who complain about their subordinates to their superiors. These people have neither real managerial experience nor knowledge of managing people at work.

It is often said that people leave managers rather than companies. And this is true because this type of manager ruins things within the department and influences things to a certain degree outside of it. Needless to say, such managers need to be avoided. Efficient and human-oriented management provides flexibility to employees, constructive feedback, and support, as well as trust or empowerment.

A common way of managing start-ups in their early stages is project management. According to the Project Management Institute,

> project management is the use of specific knowledge, skills, tools and techniques to deliver something of value to people. The development of software for an improved business process, the construction of a building, the relief effort after a natural disaster, the expansion of sales into a new geographic market – these are all examples of projects.

In other words, project management is the application of specialized information, abilities, and methods to the completion of a task for the benefit of others. Experts in the field of project management use a wide range of knowledge and abilities to inspire and direct team members toward success. It's no secret that businesses are always on the lookout for skilled project managers to assist them in completing their initiatives successfully. Creating new software to update an existing corporate process or constructing a new bridge or a building and even numerous web sources such as torrent websites and online applications are examples of projects that might be undertaken to enhance a company's operations.

Siemens Healthineers, a healthcare leader, is one of the most popular companies using project management. At any fixed instant, Siemens Healthineers oversees roughly 100 separate initiatives. In the past, SharePoint websites and groups were used to keep tabs on productivity. However, the company hoped to enhance the system for more efficient project management. Siemens Healthineers incorporated different structured project templates. Using templates, each new project can be launched consistently, thus boosting transparency. The software prioritizes milestone trend analysis, which monitors milestone progress. BrightWork lets project managers track project milestones throughout time. If the project managers fall behind, they can catch up.

After implementing BrightWork's AI-powered analytics, Siemens Healthineers achieved:

- 22% reduction in project delays.
- 15% improvement in resource utilization.
- €1.2M annual savings through predictive risk modeling.

As a project manager, you might need to investigate each aspect of the environment that constitutes project management, such as organizing, monitoring, documenting, team development, leadership, interactions, and inspiration. This involves discovering effective answers for your real-world difficulties via interaction with renowned professionals and with your peers.

Project management is also a part of everyday life, whether in personal routine or professional space. For instance, if your project is to renovate your house, it requires detailed steps and techniques of project management. Following these steps can give a clear direction to the homeowner to renovate and decorate the house:

- Making the complete list of tasks and deliverables, such as electrical work, plumbing, flooring, ceiling, and kitchen.
- Establishing deadlines and schedules for each task.
- Assigning the task to particular resources, such as carpenters, painters, and constructors.
- Monitoring the tasks with time.
- Ensuring that contingency plans are in place for anything going off course.

These days, it's common knowledge that workers in all sorts of professions may benefit from learning the fundamentals of project management. A young kid working on a scientific project may benefit from project management skills just as much as a business executive seeking to resolve personality conflicts. A nurse with these abilities may more efficiently manage shift changes, which can then speed up the ward's feedback times for patients. Whether it's an IT pro speeding up the delivery of cutting-edge software or a government agency cutting costs without sacrificing quality, these tools are invaluable.

Project management, at a glance, specifies the deliverables and the schedule for delivering them. However, a closer look reveals that the project's objectives are made clear to the whole team thanks to the efforts of the project manager, leading to pinpoint accuracy in the project's implementation.

Most of the labor involved in managing projects consists of producing useful project documentation, as most initiatives are nothing more than goals for management. On the other hand, to provide useful documentation, project planners focus their efforts on the use cases, requirements, functions, and technicalities of the project. As a result, having this documentation helps throughout the project's lifespan and assists the entire team in working appropriately. Good documentation is created because of diligent project management, and this documentation plays an essential part in explaining the essential components and basics of the project.

While management in organizations is an ongoing process with no deadline, project management has a limited lifespan and specific deliverables, which were agreed upon with the beneficiary.

One might ask why a project might fail. Well, there are a few clear reasons, and by knowing them, we can pay more attention and develop needed skills in those areas. These reasons are:

- Unrealistic planning, meaning that not all the needed resources were identified; the costs will also increase when additional resources need to be brought urgently and often while the project has started.
- Unclear objectives mean that involved people do not understand the direction and needs to be achieved; using SMART objectives is highly recommended.
- Ineffective communication can happen for many reasons; a great manager should have effective communication skills and the ability to communicate to everyone involved their expected input and in which parameters.

A project is considered a failure when it does not deliver what was required within the specified objectives, budget, and time.

A business plan often fails upon the first contact with customers. A business plan is a live document that needs to be adapted and revised as needed.

The Lean start-up methodology came as a solution to such cases. The Lean methodology is all about speed – the speed of testing a product, speed to enter the market with a minimum viable product (MVP), speed of improving and re-launching the product, and so on.

According to Eric Ries (the promoter of the Lean method), the Lean start-up methodology has four basic principles[3]:

1. *Entrepreneurship is management.* Any business enterprise needs management. And not just management but effective management and a fast learning orientation.
2. *Entrepreneurs are practically everywhere.* Every person has the potential to become an entrepreneur. But to succeed, one must learn and develop oneself on a permanent basis. Entrepreneurship starts with the person, the human being behind the enterprise.
3. *Validated learning.* A Lean start-up company offers customers a minimum viable product according to their needs. The organization will experiment through received feedback, continuous improvements, and updates/upgrades until the best solution is reached.
4. *Innovation accountability.* A Lean start-up company keeps detailed evidence of tests, product improvements, feedback, and positive and negative experiences. It focuses on what it learned about innovation.
5. *Build-measure-learn cycle.* The Lean start-up will test the MVP through customers' feedback. Once feedback is received, it is assessed, and, if required, it goes into improving the product and releasing it again on the market for testing.

An MVP is defined as the simplest version of a product that meets the consumers' needs. Using the Lean system and the minimum viable product, a company minimizes risks and potential costs. An MVP is usually released in a limited quantity to test the market and control losses if the endeavor fails.

The Gantt chart is a very practical tool for keeping track of projects and tasks' progress. It is helpful to employ Gantt charts since they display a project's operations and progression. In the chart, one can set the inability to begin a task until another element is completed, work on several tasks in parallel, or visualize any particular situation in the chart. This information can help management in gaining more in-depth knowledge of the issues that a project is up against and guide them in the process of making crucial decisions on how to proceed with a project, task, or unforeseen delays.

It is possible for those in charge of a project and those participating in it to utilize a Gantt chart to monitor the actions, deadlines, and overall process. The chart can highlight any potential constraints or problems, providing the leaders of the initiative and the participants with the ability to make modifications as required. A Gantt chart gives those who are directly responsible and/or involved with the project, as well as others with less participation, such as executives and other stakeholders, a clear perspective on deadlines, tasks, and progress.

Project managers can work together more effectively to boost output thanks to the use of Gantt charts. The high visibility provided by a Gantt chart enables involved parties to maintain their concentration on the activities that require completion. This transparency also ensures that everyone on the team[4] is responsible for the tasks assigned to them.

A Gantt chart is a graphic depiction of how tasks in a project may overlap with one another. In addition to this, it illustrates how the beginning of one task may be dependent on the conclusion of another one. Data of this kind gives project managers the ability to schedule work and distribute resources in a manner that does not impede the forward movement of the project.

The use of Gantt charts in the field of project management is by far their most widespread use. Gantt charts are crucial for planning any kind of task. They are useful graphics that assist in breaking down the strategic plan and activities on a weekly or monthly basis to ensure that the tasks are finished before the deadline.

For example, the following image shows the Gantt chart created for a house renovation project. All the tasks required for the completion of the project are shown, which can make the steps easier for the users of this chart. The start and end dates for the project, broken down into each task, can help track the progress of every activity in the given timeframe.

To craft a Gantt chart specific to your situation, a list of the tasks that need to be completed is plotted along the y-axis, and the x-axis displays how long each task will take to complete. As you add activities, start and end times, and interconnections, the colors in the bar chart will reflect your changes.

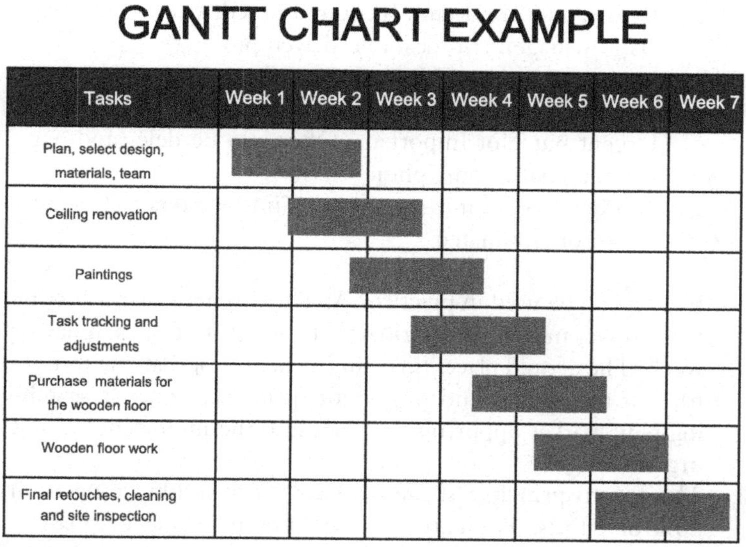

Figure 5.1 Gantt chart example for a house repair project.

Excel can be used to produce many Gantt charts. If you decide to construct your Gantt charts with Gantt chart software rather than with the framework for a Gantt chart in Excel, you will be able to do more than simply view the lengths of tasks and the dates on which they are due. You can establish a structure for work breakdown with Gantt chart tools, delegate responsibilities to individuals on your team, monitor the project's progress instantaneously, and use drag-and-drop functionality to immediately alter your timeline.

This section would be incomplete without discussing time management techniques. Effective time management is a critical skill for entrepreneurs, directly impacting their productivity, decision-making, and overall business success. So let's have a look at the core time management theories and techniques, as well as at some examples on how these can be used in practice.

1. The Eisenhower matrix, popularized by Stephen Covey, categorizes tasks based on their urgency and importance. This method helps entrepreneurs prioritize effectively by dividing tasks into four quadrants:

a. Urgent and Important: Require immediate attention (e.g., crisis management, deadline-driven projects).
b. Important but Not Urgent: Contribute to long-term success (e.g., strategic planning, skill development).
c. Urgent but Not Important: Often can be delegated (e.g., certain emails, some phone calls).
d. Neither Urgent nor Important: Time-wasters to be minimized or eliminated.

How it can be used in practice? An entrepreneur might use the Eisenhower matrix to prioritize tasks at the start of each day or week. They could place 'finalizing a client proposal due tomorrow' in the urgent and important quadrant, while 'researching new market opportunities' goes into the important but not urgent category.

2. The Pareto principle suggests that 80% of results come from 20% of efforts. For entrepreneurs, this principle emphasizes focusing on high-impact activities that drive the most significant outcomes.

   How it can be used in practice? An entrepreneur might analyze their sales data and discover that 80% of their revenue comes from 20% of their clients. This insight could lead them to allocate more time and resources to nurturing relationships and develop more partnerships with these key clients and seeking similar high-value prospects.
3. Time blocking involves allocating specific time periods for different activities throughout the day. This technique helps entrepreneurs maintain focus and reduce context-switching. I use an email program's calendar to do so and to keep track of and easy manage daily tasks.

   How it can be used in practice? An entrepreneur might block out 9 AM to 11 AM each day for focused work on strategic initiatives, 11 AM to 12 PM for responding to emails, and 1 PM to 3 PM for client meetings. Personal matters could be also included in the calendar for a better work–life balance and management.
4. The pomodoro technique involves working in focused 25-minute intervals (called 'pomodoros'), followed by short breaks. This method helps maintain concentration and prevents burnout.

How it can be used in practice? An entrepreneur working on a complex financial analysis might use the pomodoro technique, focusing intensely for 25 minutes, then taking a 5-minute break to refresh before starting the next pomodoro.

5. The ALPEN method was developed by Lothar J. Seiwert. The ALPEN method involves five steps:

   Step 1: Activities: List tasks for the day
   Step 2: Length: Estimate time for each task
   Step 3: Planning buffer: Allow 40% of time for unexpected tasks
   Step 4: Establish priorities
   Step 5: Note results and transfer unfinished items

   How it can be used in practice? An entrepreneur might start their day by listing tasks, estimating 2 hours for a strategy meeting, 3 hours for product development, and 1 hour for administrative work. They would then add a 2.4-hour buffer (40% of 6 hours), prioritize the tasks, and adjust as needed throughout the day.

The next question is: How do we implement effective time management strategies? Some recommendations are presented here:

1. Prioritization and Goal Setting: Successful entrepreneurs prioritize tasks by identifying what is most important and aligning activities with overarching business objectives. This involves:

   - Setting clear, specific goals (both short-term and long-term)
   - Breaking down large projects into manageable tasks

Technique	**Entrepreneurial Application**	**Digital Tool Pairing**
Eisenhower Matrix	Prioritize investor meetings vs. product testing	Todoist (Priority Labels)
ALPEN Method	Sprint planning for app launches	ClickUp Time Tracking
Pomodoro	Deep work sessions for patent filings	Focus@Will (Neural Focus Music)

- Focusing on high-impact activities that drive business growth

2. Delegation and Automation: Entrepreneurs must learn to delegate tasks effectively and leverage automation to free up time for strategic activities. This includes:
    - Identifying tasks that can be handled by team members or outsourced
    - Utilizing customer relationship management (CRM) tools to automate marketing and lead generation
    - Implementing project management software to streamline workflows

3. Minimizing Distractions: Reducing distractions is crucial for maintaining focus and productivity. Strategies include:
    - Creating a dedicated workspace free from interruptions
    - Using website blockers or app limits during focused work periods
    - Implementing 'do not disturb' times for deep work sessions

There is no right or wrong method or technique. Each entrepreneur should test and choose the most effective one for his or her own. Some tips for effective time management implementation:

1. Start your day early to tackle important tasks before distractions arise.
2. Use time tracking apps to gain insights into how you spend your time.
3. Implement the '2-minute rule': If a task takes less than 2 minutes, do it immediately.
4. Practice saying 'no' to non-essential commitments that don't align with your goals.
5. Utilize the 'eat the frog' technique by tackling your most challenging task first thing in the morning.
6. Create a knowledge base or standard operating procedures to streamline recurring tasks.
7. Regularly review and adjust your time management strategies to ensure continued effectiveness.

By implementing a combination of established theories, advanced strategies, and practical tips, entrepreneurs can optimize their productivity, make better decisions, and achieve their business objectives more efficiently. The key lies in consistently applying these techniques, regularly assessing their effectiveness, and adapting them to suit individual working styles and business needs.

Having established operational frameworks, financial acumen becomes the lifeblood sustaining these systems – let's examine monetary fundamentals. One can often hear that the most common objection related to starting a business is the money or the capital. Getting the capital to finance a business can be extremely difficult in the current volatile economic context[5] where cash is very scarce. You do not need to be discouraged, as these useful suggestions will offer some perspective about the resources related to financing businesses.

1. *Get a loan from a bank* – Despite the fact that the lending process is becoming more difficult, getting a bank loan to finance a business is still a good option. There are some banks that have set aside some funds to help small businesses and start-ups. You can approach the banks in your area with your business plan (budget included) to ask for a loan. Different banks have different documentation requirements, but all will ask for a detailed business plan.
2. *Use your credit card balance* – This is another option for you if you want to raise some money for your business. It allows you credit facilities in advance to help you start up. However, you should be very careful if you must use the credit card. It is not advisable for you to pay just the minimum payment every month or fail to pay for some months. This will affect your credit score negatively. Therefore, try not to fail in your monthly payment and make sure that you pay more than the minimum monthly payment to be on the safe side.
3. *Get a loan from the SME[6] authority in your country or European non-refundable grants if you are in Europe* – Because of the economic challenges we are currently facing and some other factors, getting a bank loan these days can be challenging. If that happens to you, you can take a loan from the SME authority or apply for non-refundable grants offered by the European

Union (if your business is located in an EU Member State). This body always has loans available to help small businesses. You can read their requirements and see if you are qualified to get a loan. If you are, rest assured that you will have sufficient loans to start up with.

4. *Seek financial assistance from your family and friends (also called 'love money')* – If you have a well-thought-out business plan, you can approach your family members and friends for assistance to help you start your business. You should have enough evidence to convince them to fund it with their money. Your plan should include a clear repayment strategy to prevent putting your personal relationship at risk. The most important thing here is to be transparent with them as far as the business is concerned. Let them be aware of potential problems that the business may face and how you plan to get out of them. If you can do this, they may be convinced to give you a shoulder to lean on.
5. *Consider a microloan* – This is another alternative to a bank loan. If all else fails, consider getting a microloan. Although microloans are usually smaller than loans from commercial banks, they will give you something to start with. Aside from that, these lenders are more considerate than most banks, have fewer documentation procedures, and charge higher interest rates than commercial banks.

Other financing options for your business could be crowdfunding, business angels, experienced investors interested in diversifying their portfolio, or some joint venture partnerships.

A very important thing that you need to remember is that the firm's money is NOT your pocket money. It means that you can't just take it out as you please.

Basic accounting knowledge will allow you to understand bank statements, financial statements, calculate costs, and other critical elements. The most commonly used terms are debit and credit (of an account, for example). Debit entries increase assets/expenses (left side), while credits increase liabilities/equity/revenue (right side) in double-entry accounting.

Pro tip: AI-Driven Accounting Alert: Modern platforms like Sage Intacct now offer real-time anomaly detection – automatically flagging expenses exceeding budget thresholds or unusual cash flow patterns.

A budget is an estimation of costs and/or income for a specified period. The budget can be monthly, biannual, yearly, and so on. In the following, you can find a budget template for a start-up. You can customize the budget based on the needs of your specific situation.

The **breakeven point** is, simply put, the point where the expenses are equal to the income. Once this point is exceeded, the firm starts making profit. There are many formulas to calculate the breakeven point, but the simple one is presented in the following, and it determines the quantity needed to be sold to reach the 'breakeven point.'

Calculation method:

Unit sale price − *Unit variable cost* = *X* (any currency)

Then, we *divide the fixed costs by X (the currency amount calculated previously) = number of units needed to be sold to cover the expenses (in the 'breakeven' point income = expenses).*

Let's look at an example of breakeven point calculation based on the quantity needed to be sold.

Jane has an online platform where she sells pajamas for kids. Her cost for one pajama (unit variable cost) is €10. She calculated her sales cost per pajama at €18 (unit sale price). Her total fixed costs are €6,000 monthly. What is the breakeven point in this case?

Calculation:

€18 (unit sale price) − €10 (unit variable cost) = €8

€6,000 (the fixed costs)/€8 = 750 pieces (the 'breakeven point,' meaning that Jane will start to have profit once she sells more than 750 pajamas)

Fixed costs are recurring monthly expenses that are approximately at the same level (even if these are paid annually or quarterly; for example, rent, some utilities, salaries, insurances, and subscriptions), while variable costs vary every month based on certain factors such

Table 5.1 Budget template for a start-up

No	Expense Category/Item	Amount Estimated (Monthly/Annually)	Source of Funds
1.	Fee or tax (firm registration)		
2.	Rent for at least the first 6 months (if needed)		
3.	Professional fees (consultant, lawyer)		
4.	Equipment (laptop, phones, car, etc.)		
5.	Supplies (office, production, etc.)		
6.	Marketing and sales budget (online promotions, prints, social media manager, etc.)		
7.	Accountant fee for the first 6 months		
8.	Insurances (if needed at start)		
9.	Salaries (gross ones, if needed) for the first 6 months		
10.	Stock acquisition and taxes (if imported)		
11.	Technology-related costs (website construction, administration, landing pages, etc.)		
12.	Other cost categories specific to your type of business		
13.	Unforeseen expenses (10% of total)		
	Total estimation		

Notes: The budget elements are general and might need customization based on the specificity of your business. When calculating it, you need to take into consideration all possible cost-incurring components at realistic values. Think broadly and detail each cost category. You can also consider rolling 13-week cash flow forecasts for early-stage ventures rather than static annual budgets to improve liquidity management.

as production level, special circumstances, and business growth. These variable costs can be electricity, water (if manufacturing is using it), raw materials, advertisements, commissions, or cost of sold goods. The categories depend largely on your commercial activity.

The variable cost per unit represents the amount of raw materials, labor, additional materials, and other resources necessary to produce it. The variable costs can increase or decrease based on the quantity of goods produced/manufactured. Another important notion is the variable cost ratio; this allows you to assess the relationship between variable costs and net sales. It is calculated by dividing the total variable costs by the net sales.[7]

The sale price can be calculated in several ways. A simple one is starting from the variable cost per unit and adding the quota from the fixed costs (total fixed costs divided by the number of products manufactured or produced), plus a reasonable margin of profit (depending on the industry, it can be from 5% to 300% or even more on the luxury market). And of course, additional taxes such as value-added tax (VAT).

Good communication with your accountant or financial specialist is essential. Following reports and advice for expenses, optimization should be a priority for you. My advice is to search for an accountant who can advise, guide, and support you regarding matters of money and finances. The digital era provides even more accounting and finance-related software; there are many with open source or free versions that are suitable for start-ups' needs.

Other terms for your consideration:[8]

Amortization is 'the gradual charging to expense of the cost of an intangible asset (such as a purchased patent) over the useful life of the asset.'

Depreciation is the 'gradual charging to expense of the cost of a tangible asset (such as production equipment) over the useful life of the asset.'

Economy of scale refers to a variety of similar products (or those from the same line) manufactured all together; in this way, they come cheaper than an individual category/sort manufacturing. Similarly, a company can make marketing strategies for all its product lines together.

Economy of scope refers to decreased price due to manufacturing a large number of products to be sold on a large market or several markets. In simple words, if one produces more pieces, the cost per unit decreases proportionally with the quantity.

Return on investment (ROI) is how one can measure the performance of the investment, in this case the profitability of the business. It can be calculated by dividing the cost of an investment (money invested in business) by the profit earned through the investment. It is expressed as a percentage. For example, if at the end of the year, one has a profit of €100,000 and the cost of investment is €25,000, then ROI represents (100,000/25,000) × 100 = 400%.

Opportunity cost represents the value of the best alternative given up. In other words, if someone spends money at a restaurant at the mall, they cannot spend the same time (and money) on dinner with family at home.

Accounting balance is the end-of-the-month centralized reports containing all the movements from the specified month; sometimes it can also contain the centralized sums from previous months.

Balance sheet is a 6-month or yearly financial statement, which is usually sent to the financial authority in your country. It centralizes everything and calculates the profit or loss for the specific period.

Deductible expenses or tax-deductible expenses are those that help the business to generate income; these are subtracted from the gross income. Depending on the specificity of each company (and country), these expenses can be fuel, insurance, marketing, maintenance and repairs, rent, salaries, utilities, or subscriptions.

Nondeductible expenses are those expenses not allowed to be subtracted from the gross revenue of the company. Such expenses (depending on countries) can be taxes, late payment penalties, personal expenses (such as dresses, shoes, makeup, and perfumes), most meals and entertainment, and travel expenses not related to business and for non-company employees.

Effective expense and tax optimization have become critical components of financial management for companies operating in Europe. This section provides a general overview of expense and tax optimization strategies tailored to the European context, taking into account the complexities of EU regulations, International Financial Reporting Standards (IFRS), and the diverse tax regimes across member states. By implementing such strategies, businesses can not only reduce costs and tax liabilities but also improve operational efficiency, ensure compliance, and create sustainable value for stakeholders. We will delve into practical, actionable advice that aligns with European accounting standards and best practices, offering a roadmap for companies seeking to optimize their financial operations in the European market. You should always seek personalized advice or keep yourself updated with the latest financial laws, as the financial regulations are frequently changing.

1. Implement Activity-Based Costing (ABC): ABC provides a more accurate allocation of overhead costs, helping identify areas for potential cost reduction. This aligns with International Financial Reporting Standards principles of fair presentation and relevance.
2. Leverage Technology for Expense Management: Implement expense management software that complies with European e-invoicing standards (Directive 2014/55/EU). This ensures accurate tracking, reduces manual errors, and facilitates compliance with VAT regulations.
3. Optimize Working Capital: Improve inventory management using just-in-time practices and negotiate better terms with suppliers. This aligns with IAS 2 (Inventories) and helps reduce carrying costs.

What about tax optimization strategies? In the following, you can find some general suggestions. These should be assessed based on the specificity of the firm, national regulations, and other economic indicators that might be applicable in the country in which your company is based.

- Utilize R&D Tax Incentive: Many European countries offer R&D tax credits. Ensure proper documentation of R&D activities to maximize these benefits, in line with IAS 38 (Intangible Assets) for capitalization of development costs.
- Implement Transfer Pricing Strategies: Develop a robust transfer pricing policy that complies with OECD guidelines and local country regulations. This is crucial for multinational companies to optimize tax liabilities across jurisdictions.

- Leverage Double Tax Treaties: Utilize the extensive network of double tax treaties within Europe to minimize withholding taxes on cross-border transactions. This requires careful structuring of international operations.
- Consider Patent Box Regimes: Several European countries offer reduced tax rates on income derived from patents and other intellectual property. Align IP management strategies with these regimes to reduce overall tax burden.

Next you can find some general tips related to your company's finances:

- Conduct regular tax health checks to ensure compliance and identify optimization opportunities.
- Invest in employee training on expense policies and tax compliance to minimize errors and potential risks.
- Stay informed about changes in European tax laws and accounting standards to proactively adapt strategies.
- Consider setting up a holding company structure in a tax-efficient jurisdiction within the EU to optimize overall group taxation.
- Implement robust documentation practices for all tax positions to withstand potential audits.

By implementing such strategies, companies can optimize their expenses and tax positions while remaining compliant with European accounting standards and regulations. Remember to consult with local tax experts for country-specific advice, as tax laws can vary significantly across Europe.

Entrepreneurship is not merely a career path – it's a mindset forged in resilience, refined by strategy, and fueled by vision. As you navigate the complex interplay of management rigor and financial acumen, remember: every spreadsheet analyzed, every project milestone met, and every customer need anticipated is a brick in the foundation of your legacy. The frameworks in this chapter are not theoretical concepts but survival tools for the modern entrepreneur – use them to turn uncertainty into opportunity, pressure into precision, and risks into rewards. Stay curious, stay lean, and let your financial discipline be the compass that steers you through storms toward sustainable growth. The world doesn't just need more businesses; it needs *your* business – the one you'll build with clarity, lead with humanity, and scale with wisdom. Now go make your mark.

NOTES

1 About 100 years ago, Henry Fayol, a French engineer, set the first 14 management principles, which were applicable during the industrial revolution and Europe's level of economic and technological development at that time. These principles were later refined and are now concentrated into these four.
2 CEO is the abbreviation for the chief executive officer or general manager of a company.
3 Adapted from Eric Reis's website, July 2022. See http://theleanstartup.com/
4 Nowadays, modern entrepreneurs often use RACI matrices (responsible, accountable, consulted, informed) to clarify roles in agile teams.
5 We can characterize the current economic context as VUCA – volatility, uncertainty, complexity, and ambiguity. Sometimes it is used as an excuse to dismiss plans and projected strategies.
6 SMEs stands for small and medium enterprises, an acronym often used in the business world.
7 The sum of a total gross sales for a specific period (usually a year) minus its returns, allowances, and discounts, if applicable.
8 Definitions from www.accountingtools.com/articles/what-are-examples-of-fixed-costs.html.

6

CLOSING THE LOOP

Practical strategies for profitable circular business models

Once a peripheral consideration, sustainability has emerged as a critical strategic priority for modern enterprises. As Porter and Kramer emphasized in their 2019 Harvard Business Review analysis, organizations that align their primary operations with addressing pressing social challenges gain significant competitive advantages in today's economic landscape.

The concept of sustainability now permeates boardroom discussions across industries. Contemporary organizations must now confront sustainability considerations – whether addressing immediate operational demands or long-term systemic pressures – to maintain relevance. While entrepreneurial motivations vary – ranging from economic autonomy to creative fulfillment – all enterprises share the fundamental requirement of maintaining viability. This imperative has spurred diverse theories on operational sustainability, particularly as market-driven systems face mounting criticism. According to Michael Porter and Mark Kramer (Harvard Business School professors) in a 2011 HBR article,

> the capitalist system is under siege. In recent years business increasingly has been viewed as a major cause of social, environmental and economic problems. Companies are widely perceived to be prospering at the expense of the broader community.[1]

Based on the significance of sustainable development to virtually all aspects of human endeavor, many theories and principles have

DOI: 10.4324/9781003591429-7

been developed, all offering some seemingly good and efficient ways in which an organization can approach the issue of organizational sustainability. Lately, many organizations have introduced or changed their policies, products, and/or processes to address pollution, optimize resource usage, and improve stakeholder and community relations. The need to replenish the source of a product is necessary for the profitability and survival of any endeavor. A business unconcerned about the future is a business whose future is uncertain. In the constantly evolving world we live in, coupled with the increasing advancements in technology, exploring the prospect of sustainable development is, therefore, an inevitable process for every business entity.

After a closer examination of the concept of sustainable development, one thing is quite noticeable, and that is the fact that sustainable development is some sort of compromise between growth and conservation, as it is clear that there is a nexus between the two. At any given time, sustainable development, when applied to any field of endeavor, curates a way of maximizing the resources of today and sustaining the resources for future use. It effectively fuses together the concept of growth and modernization both in the short and long term. However, just like in most issues of global importance, there are distinctive views about the concept of sustainability, especially as it applies to the business setting. This is why some organizations are not fully invested in the idea of incorporating principles of sustainability into their business operations. For instance, some stakeholders are of the view that sustainability in its complete form and development in its total form are a bit contradictory, as an organization is certainly going to have to sacrifice to choose one rather than pursue the two at the same time.

Adopting a hard stance on sustainability will often result in lower profits in the present but an improved profit margin in the future. This is because, for most organizations, there would be a need to adopt several measures that will reduce waste and pollution. And with the increasing drive toward reducing gaseous emissions from manufacturing organizations, some of the available greenhouse alternatives will invariably result in lower yield, albeit with a positive effect on the environment.

Economic development always brings about further advancements in how humans get things done. Evidently, there has been a major change between the culture, norms, and beliefs of people of this century and those that lived many centuries ago. It is evidently clear that the standard of living today is higher than what was obtained three centuries ago. However, the same technology that made life easier is the same that has led to the depletion of the ecosystem.

Every day, as wood is being cut in the jungles to make furniture for humans and gases are being flared by big organizations worldwide, we are effectively weakening the ecosystem, which will become unsustainable in the next few decades if care is not taken. Also, economic development has brought about a more severe gap between the rich and the poor in some societies rather than bridging the gap between them. This could very much bring about a series of challenges for these nations.

There are certain principles guiding the implementation of sustainable development in companies; therefore, companies interested in making their organizations compliant with sustainable development ideals must do sustainability implementation side by side with their organization's threats and opportunities. Hence, the sustainable development strategies adopted by organizations will differ from one to the other. However, whatever the case, certain steps are pertinent to be undertaken by any organization interested in adopting sustainable development measures. The first step is to assess the current reality and projected trends. The size and capacity of an organization will have a strong impact on its capacity of the scope of its operations. For instance, there are organizations with global scope; these are organizations whose scope extends beyond the geographical boundaries of a country. The operations of these organizations with a global perspective will take into consideration the extant laws and cultures of the countries of their operations. Likewise, the production capacity of these organizations would be bigger and more diverse than those whose scope is limited to one country or perhaps a state or two.

Assessing current reality and projected trends is another step to be taken. This is premised upon the realization that trends determine sales. As the world continues to undergo a technological revolution, machines have transformed how products are manufactured and services are rendered. Hence, as new products are manufactured at intervals, new services are also being fashioned to complement one another. This development has had a remarkable influence on the demand patterns of the final consumer.

A company that does not factor projected trends into its system of operations is going through a slippery slope that can have severe consequences on its operations, even in the short term. Take the example of the Finnish company Nokia. For several decades, Nokia was one of the globally renowned mobile phone makers, and the majority of its phones were built with Java and Symbian technology, with a few of its products also coming with Windows technology. However, as the world gradually advanced toward Android technology, Nokia initially dominated the mobile market with Symbian and Windows-based devices. However, its delayed adoption of Android technology led to a rapid decline. By 2013, Nokia's mobile division was acquired by Microsoft, illustrating the consequences of ignoring market trends.'

This is perfect evidence of the importance and relevance of projected trends to the sustainability of any organization. Top organizations make considerable investments by investigating future consumer behavior to align their services and offerings to meet these needs. This way, they would be able to sustain their profitability and stay well above the competition.

Regarding defining a compelling vision of what the company wants to create, each company in operation in any economy has its own mission, purpose, and objectives. These goals and objectives form the guiding principles to which they align their operations, and this forms the yardstick upon which members of staff are evaluated, compensated, and rewarded. Leadership is a huge aspect of the viability and profitability of every organization, as it is the major determinant of the direction the company takes. The task of coordinating all activities of the firm rests squarely on the shoulders of the leaders, and this is why most top organizations also have good leadership. In fact, in the final analysis, in most cases, the difference between successful organizations and not-so-successful ones is always a function of leadership. The leadership must establish a compelling vision for the organization and must relate the same to the workforce in clear and unambiguous terms. This is because they must lead for others to follow. The passion and zeal with which they outline the company's objectives are directly proportional to how much importance will be attached to them by the members of the workforce.

Every organization in pursuit of sustainable development must be interested in establishing a set of measurable results geared toward the achievement of the vision. It is good to be ambitious and aim high, but it is even more important to set achievable goals, and then, as the goals are achieved, newer, tougher goals can be achieved. The importance of this comes from the fact that when a goal too high is set and it is not met, the motivation of that organization's personnel is immediately weakened, and their self-belief is reduced due to their inability to achieve the earlier target set. Hence the best strategy that any organization can adopt has to be to start small and then aim higher. Motivation is very important because it determines the level of output, and the interesting thing about motivation is that it can be built up, and the best way to build up motivation is to adopt the bottom-up approach. The greater the task accomplished, the more confidence is built up. When the personnel of the organization meet their targets, the management must motivate them to do more. This will create healthy competition, which will bring about innovation and increased output in the organization.

Designing a strategy to bridge the gap between where you are as an organization today and where you want to be in the future will facilitate the implementation of a sustainability strategy that will benefit the organization. Setting a goal brings about a sense of duty on the enormity of the task that needs to be accomplished and helps the personnel of the organization coordinate all activities needed to achieve the set goal. It takes strategy to plan, and planning is needed by every organization.

Strategic sustainable management is the 'new fashion' nowadays. The quest to ensure the creation of any sustainable system, as well as the modification of a current structure to become sustainable, requires an influx of needed tools that will guide the process from the onset to its final completion.

The benefits that are accruable to any sustainable management process are numerous and affect a wide range of individuals. For instance:

1. It safeguards the preservation of the ecosystem. Every sustainable management process that provides excellent waste management, as well as reduction of energy and water consumption, will ultimately reduce the carbon footprint that

would be left by humans, and these safeguard the planet from pending disaster.

2. It provides solutions to dire human challenges. In the long run, sustainable management brings cheap solutions to the challenges that societies face. One such challenge is the provision of good electricity for all parts of the world, most especially within third world countries. This challenge drove the research that brought solar photovoltaic panels into existence and continues to drive research for other forms of renewable energy.

Different countries are investing *en masse* in sustainable companies to ensure the buildup of sustainable structures. This is obtainable because the government recognizes the benefits of sustainable growth that are achieved when the economy grows without encountering newer economic problems for future generations.

As declared by the World Economic Forum, the circular economy promotes efficient usage of natural resources, waste elimination, and transition to net-zero industry. In a traditional, systemic approach, unprocessed materials are extracted, manufactured, and then discarded. On the other hand, the goal of the circular economy model is to reduce the separation between human output and the natural variability of habitats. However, this also entails banking

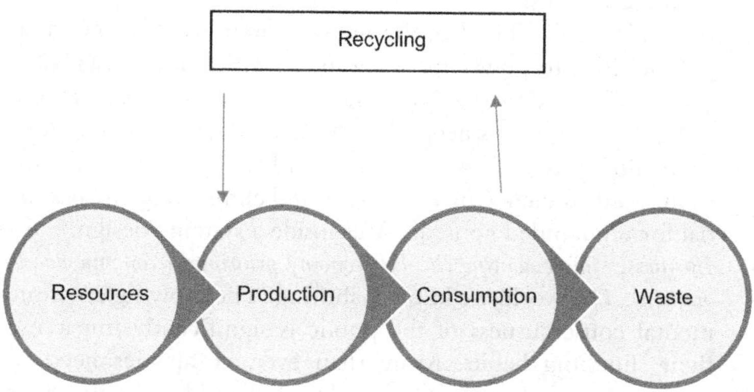

Figure 6.1 The circular economy system.

on renewable sources of energy and abandoning the usage of chemical substances.

THE MAIN PRINCIPLES OF THE CIRCULAR ECONOMY

The circular economy represents a transformative model for breaking the link between economic expansion and resource depletion. Departing from the environmentally taxing 'produce-use-discard' linear approach, this framework prioritizes regenerative cycles where products and materials circulate continuously through repair, refurbishment, and reprocessing (as illustrated in Figure 6.1).

1. *Eliminating Pollution and Waste*: Central to this model is the principle that waste becomes an obsolete concept. Products are engineered for extended lifespans using durable materials, coupled with intentional design for disassembly and material recovery. This dual focus enables seamless reintroduction of components into production streams, minimizing energy-intensive processing. Unlike conventional recycling – which often downgrades materials – the circular approach preserves value through tiered renewal strategies, from component reuse to molecular-level reengineering.
2. *Maintaining the usage cycle of products and materials*: One goal of the circular economy is to keep goods, parts, and raw materials at peak efficiency for as long as possible to maximize resource returns.
3. *Renewable energy*: The last premise of a circular economy is that the fuel used to power the economy comes from a sustainable source. This is done to reduce reliance on finite resources and strengthen the robustness of the broader economic and environmental systems that sustain human life. This approach aims to increase efficiency by identifying and eliminating any potential for unintended consequences inside a system's design.
4. *Businesses implementing circular economy principles (economic development)*: The world we know is shifting. The growing environmental consciousness of the public is significantly impacting their shopping habits. More than ever, companies need to adjust their operations to include circular ideas across their entire distribution networks.

The following steps can be taken for this purpose:

> When creating new items or containers, a corporation should bear in mind the importance of longevity, renewability, and reuse to maintain the flow of materials and elements throughout the system. This is the recycling concept that is being adopted by companies.

The demand for ecologically responsible shipping, production, and goods within our community has never been higher than it is today because 8 million tons of plastic are dumped into our seas yearly. It is time to adjust your mindset regarding the materials you use, either by considering switching to ones that are simply recyclable or by investigating whether resources inside your company may be recycled for other uses.

Regenerating and refreshing natural systems are important since there is no wastage in the natural world. Yet every year, the globe disposes of millions of tons of materials that might be used to replenish important nutrients in the soil, allowing us to reduce our reliance on potentially hazardous substances.

Let's take a look at the example of takeout meals packages. The packing of takeout meals presents a difficulty from a sustainability standpoint, even though this type of dining is quite profitable. Burger King, a brand in the world of fast-food takeout, introduced a remedy in the shape of recycled plastic, intending to reduce the volume of wastage that it creates. This stops the cycle of creating and dumping waste after the consumption of food and incorporates the process of recycling. The strategy, which will be implemented for 2023, calls for the customer to pay a preliminary cash fee, which will then be reimbursed when they return the cartons and glasses, which are then removed for cleanup and handling via the zero-waste e-commerce program known as Loop. This step is, again, taken to reduce the waste created by the company's items and to create awareness among consumers.

According to the 2024 BK Sustainability Report, by 2024, Burger King reported a 34% reduction in single-use packaging across participating EU markets, with 81% of customers returning containers.

This chapter would be incomplete without a discussion about the SDGs and sustainability reporting. The SDGs can be considered a strategic imperative for business. The United Nations SDGs, adopted in 2015, represent a critical framework for addressing global challenges. Let's look into the impact of the SDGs on business practices in developed economies, focusing on Europe, the USA, and Canada, and provide evidence-based strategies for their implementation.

As revealed in the 2024 UN's SDG Showcase report, businesses participating in SDGs achieve market differentiation, expansion, and new business opportunities. That sets the economic rationale for embedding SDGs into a company's strategy.

While all 17 SDGs are interconnected, four goals hold more interest and applicability for businesses in the first world:

1. SDG 13 (Climate Action): In essence, this will become a long-term necessity to sustain business operations.
2. SDG 9: Industry, Innovation, and Infrastructure: These drive competitiveness and growth.
3. SDG 12: Responsible Consumption and Production: These improve resource efficiency.
4. SDG 8: Decent Work and Economic Growth: These foster sustainable economic models.

Let's look at some successful implementations of SDGs:

1. Integration of SDGs Into Core Business Strategy: The Sustainable Living Plan of Unilever (Netherlands/UK) aligns with the SDGs, creating a driver for innovation and growth. Unilever's Sustainable Living brands grew 69% faster than others in 2019 (a 2024 UN report shows a sustained 12% annual growth since 2020).
2. Circular Economy Adoption: Interface is a US-based company providing global commercial flooring. The adoption of the circular economy model follows the principles of SDG 12. Since 1995, their ReEntry program has kept more than 309 million pounds of carpet out of landfills.
3. Renewable Energy Transition: Ørsted of Denmark was an oil and gas company that changed its business model toward renewable energy, thus aligning with SDGs 7 and 13. In 2019, the generation of energy by Ørsted was from renewable sources at 85%, with a target to increase it to 99% by 2025.

4. Innovative Product Development: Beyond Meat's alternative plant-based meat (USA) contributes to the achievement of SDGs 12 and 13 by minimizing the footprint of food production on the environment. Their products require 99% less water and 93% less land compared to beef production.
5. Partnerships for the Goals (SDG 17): The Ocean Cleanup, a non-profit organization from the Netherlands, partners with corporations like Maersk and Deloitte to develop technologies for removing plastic waste from oceans, addressing SDG 14 (Life Below Water).

These implementations can't be performed without some quantifiable metrics to track the progress. Such metrics could be setting science-based targets aligned with SDGs, frameworks like TCFD for comprehensive reporting and implementation of regular sustainability audits.

Some tips for effective SDG implementation:

1. The SDG Compass tool developed by GRI, UN Global Compact, and WBCSD is a step-by-step guide.
2. Adoption of internal carbon pricing to make decarbonization efforts real.
3. Designing compensation for executives that is directly linked to the SDGs.
4. Formation of cross-functional SDG task forces for proper integration into the organization.
5. Use of digital technologies such as AI and blockchain to improve measurement and reporting on SDGs.
6. Take part in industry-wide initiatives addressing SDGs, such as the Sustainable Apparel Coalition or the Global Food Safety Initiative.
7. Regular 'SDG innovation sprints' for ideating new SDG-aligned products or processes.

SDGs present a holistic approach to the enhanced sustainability performance of businesses for unlocking new avenues of growth. Businesses in advanced economies can make a meaningful difference in their contribution toward these global goals if SDGs are strategically integrated into the core operations, fostering innovation and leveraging cross-sector partnerships. As we head towards 2030, companies need to speed up their SDG efforts, as their long-term success is irretrievably linked to global sustainable development. The examples from Europe, the USA, and Canada demonstrate that SDG alignment is not only possible but can drive substantial business value while contributing to urgent global challenges.

Like any other framework, there are also considerable criticisms against the SDGs. The following summary outlines some of the major critiques:

1. Growth contradiction: While the SDGs call for environmental sustainability, they also promote economic growth, which many feel is incompatible.
2. Poverty reduction: Critics argue that economic growth, as promoted by the SDGs, does not necessarily reduce poverty.
3. Non-binding nature: The SDGs are not underpinned by any effective accountability mechanism, which in effect renders them a set of wishes rather than binding goals.
4. Underfunding: The gap between the resources required and the resources allocated for the SDGs is very large.
5. Lack of urgency: According to many, the timeline for 2030 is not ambitious enough considering the pressing nature of global challenges.
6. Data deficiencies: There's a lack of reliable data to measure progress, and some countries may manipulate statistics.
7. Goal overload: With 17 goals and numerous targets, critics argue that the SDGs lack focus and prioritization.
8. Rights vs. goals approach: By setting goals instead of rights, the SDGs may allow leaders to claim progress without addressing fundamental issues.
9. Inequality exacerbation potential: The SDGs are at risk of increasing the disparity in both between and within nations.
10. Lack of focus on local context: Also, there is criticism that goals ignore local contexts, which seems top-down.

These criticisms are largely justified, as they point to real challenges and limitations of the SDG framework. However, it's important to note that the SDGs also represent a significant global effort to address pressing issues and have driven some positive change. The critiques should be seen as opportunities for improving the approach to sustainable development rather than reasons to abandon the goals entirely. According to 2024 UNGC report, despite these limitations, the SDGs have mobilized unprecedented cross-sector collaboration. Over 15,000 companies globally now align strategies with the goals, driving $12 trillion in annual market opportunities.

The next area of discussion is sustainability reporting and the new European standards. The landscape of sustainability reporting is undergoing a significant transformation with the introduction of the Corporate Sustainability Reporting Directive (CSRD). This analysis examines the key changes and implications for businesses and provides practical strategies for effective implementation.

The Corporate Sustainability Reporting Directive, effective from January 2023, represents a paradigm shift in sustainability reporting within the European Union. It expands the scope of companies required to report on sustainability matters from 12,000 companies under the previous Non-Financial Reporting Directive (NFRD) to approximately 50,000 companies. This includes large companies and listed SMEs.

Key changes include to the new sustainability reporting include an expanded scope of reporting, introduction of European Sustainability Reporting Standards (ESRS), a requirement for double materiality assessments, mandatory external verification, and specific digital reporting format requirements.

The European Sustainability Reporting Standards, developed by EFRAG, provide a comprehensive framework for sustainability reporting. These standards are tailored to EU policies while aligning with international initiatives. They include cross-cutting standards, environmental standards, social standards, and governance standards.

The CSRD, adopted in January 2023, phases in reporting requirements:

- 2024: Large public-interest companies (500+ employees).
- 2025: Companies with 250+ employees or €40M revenue.
- 2026: Specified SMEs.

Practical implementation strategies are listed as follows:

1. Double Materiality Assessment: Companies must conduct thorough double materiality assessments to identify sustainability issues that are material from both financial and impact perspectives. This involves:

    - Impact materiality: Assessing material topics related to sustainability matters such as carbon emissions, workforce diversity, and human rights
    - Financial materiality: Focusing on sustainability matters likely to affect a company's financial performance

2. Data Collection and Management: Implement robust data management systems to streamline the collection and reporting of sustainability information. Many companies (nearly three-quarters) still rely on spreadsheets for sustainability reporting, which may not be sufficient for the increased complexity of CSRD requirements.
3. Cross-Functional Collaboration: Establish sustainability reporting teams that include representatives from various business functions. On average, eight business functions and departments are involved in CSRD implementation, including sustainability (93%), finance (77%), and executive committee and board (73% and 72%, respectively).
4. Alignment with ESRS: Ensure reporting aligns with the ESRS, which provides a comprehensive and comparable framework for ESG disclosure. This includes understanding and implementing the specific requirements for each relevant standard.
5. External Assurance Preparation: Prepare for increased scrutiny by developing internal controls and documentation processes that can withstand external scrutiny. The CSRD requires sustainability information to be verified by an independent third party.

Tips for effective sustainability reporting:

1. Start early: Begin preparing for new reporting requirements well in advance of mandatory deadlines.

Challenges	Opportunities
1. Data quality and availability (cited as a top barrier to CSRD implementation) 2. Complexity of new reporting requirements, especially for companies new to sustainability reporting 3. Integration of sustainability information into financial decision-making processes	1. Enhanced transparency and stakeholder trust 2. Improved risk management and strategic planning 3. Access to sustainable finance and investment opportunities 4. Potential for revenue growth and cost savings (38% of companies reporting in 2025 anticipate revenue growth from CSRD implementation)

2. Invest in technology: Implement robust data management systems to streamline data collection and reporting processes.
3. Engage stakeholders: Align reporting with stakeholder priorities and engage them throughout the process.
4. Focus on material issues: Conduct thorough double materiality assessments to identify the most relevant sustainability topics for your company.
5. Ensure data accuracy: Conduct gap analyses to identify areas where information is missing and improve data collection and validation processes.
6. Adopt EU-recognized standards: Develop a strong understanding of EU-aligned reporting requirements and frameworks like the ESRS and EU Sustainability Taxonomy.
7. Prepare for assurance: Develop internal controls and documentation processes that can withstand external verification.

The CSRD and associated reporting standards represent a significant evolution in corporate sustainability disclosure. While challenging, this new era of reporting offers opportunities for companies to enhance their sustainability performance, improve stakeholder engagement, and drive long-term value creation. By proactively embracing these new standards and developing robust reporting processes, companies can not only meet regulatory requirements but also position themselves as leaders in corporate sustainability.

The pursuit of sustainability is no longer a choice but a strategic imperative for survival and relevance in the 21st-century economy.

As this chapter has shown – through pioneers like Ørsted's renewable transition, Unilever's Sustainable Living Brands, and Burger King's Loop initiative – businesses that harmonize profit with planetary boundaries are not just safeguarding ecosystems but redefining competitive advantage. The frameworks we've explored – from the circular economy's closed-loop systems to the SDGs' global blueprint and the CSRD's rigorous reporting – are not constraints but catalysts for innovation. Criticisms of these systems remind us that perfection is a process, not a destination. As we advance toward 2030 and beyond, let this be our call to action: Every policy adjusted, every supply chain audited, and every executive compensation plan tied to sustainability metrics is a brick in the foundation of a resilient future. The companies that thrive will be those that recognize sustainability not as a cost but as the ultimate driver of value, trust, and legacy. The challenge is immense, but so is the opportunity – to build enterprises that don't just adapt to the future but actively shape it.

NOTE

1 Link to the original article published in Harvard Business Review, nr. R1101C, January 2011: https://hbr.org/2011/01/the-big-idea-creating-shared-value

7

DIGITAL DARWINISM

Surviving the marketing evolution with Rogers' theory

The marketing department or area is a vital one for any organization. Marketing is handling sales that bring revenue and implicit customers to the company. Without customers, organizations cannot exist.

Marketing (the traditional one) is the complex activities taken by an organization to promote and sell its products or services. It includes advertising, market research, and product delivery. Digital marketing, instead, represents the promotion of a product/service or brand over the internet. Digital marketing enables real-time campaign analytics, allowing swift optimization of underperforming tactics. Digital marketing makes use of web-based channels to communicate with customers or potential customers. Simply put, digital marketing is a section of digital marketing.

The 4Ps of marketing, form the foundation of any successful marketing strategy. Developed by E. Jerome McCarthy in 1960, this framework consists of product, price, place, and promotion. Each element plays a crucial role in shaping how a company markets its offerings to target consumers. Let's explore each component and provide practical examples of their application.

Product: refers to the good or service being offered to consumers. It encompasses all aspects of what is being sold, including features, design, quality, and branding. To exemplify this, Apple meticulously designs its iPhones with cutting-edge features, sleek

DOI: 10.4324/9781003591429-8

aesthetics, and high-quality materials. The company focuses on user experience, continually improving functionality and introducing innovative technologies like Face ID and advanced camera systems.

Price: represents the amount customers pay for the product. It involves strategies such as pricing models, discounts, and payment terms. An example of this component is Netflix offering different subscription tiers (Basic, Standard, Premium) at varying price points. This strategy allows them to cater to different customer segments based on their willingness to pay and desired features, such as video quality and number of simultaneous streams.

Place: refers to where and how the product is made available to customers. It includes distribution channels, logistics, and market coverage. The best example here is Amazon. Amazon has revolutionized the concept of place with its vast distribution network. The company utilizes strategically located fulfilment centers, partnerships with local delivery services, and innovative solutions like Amazon Lockers to ensure products are readily available to customers across various locations.

Promotion: encompasses all communication efforts to inform, persuade, and remind customers about the product. It includes advertising, public relations, and sales promotions. The best example here is Coca-Cola's 'Share a Coke' campaign. The campaign personalized bottles with popular names and phrases, encouraging customers to find and share bottles with friends and family. This promotion leveraged social media, word-of-mouth marketing, and traditional advertising to create a highly engaging and successful marketing initiative.

Unlike traditional marketing, digital one refers to the promotion of products or services through various forms of electronic media, primarily on the internet. It utilizes online channels to engage target audiences through strategies like content marketing, social media advertising, email campaigns, and search engine optimization (SEO). It has become the standard since COVID and it is likely to remain that way.

Key aspects of digital marketing include:

1. Targeted Approach: Unlike traditional marketing, digital marketing targets specific audience segments, often identified by demographics and behaviors.
2. Data-Driven Strategies: Digital marketing works by targeting customers through data-driven strategies across digital channels like websites, search engines, social media platforms, and email.
3. Real-Time Measurement: It allows businesses to measure results in real time, making it one of the most effective ways to grow a business, increase brand awareness, and generate revenue.
4. Multiple Channels: Digital marketing encompasses various types of strategies, including:
    - Search engine optimization.
    - Pay-per-click advertising (PPC).
    - Social media marketing.
    - Content marketing.
    - Email marketing.
5. Cost-Effectiveness: Digital marketing offers cost-effective options for businesses of all sizes, allowing them to choose strategies that align with their financial capacity.
6. Global Reach: It enables businesses to extend their audience worldwide, connecting with customers from various regions.
7. Flexibility and Adaptability: Digital marketing allows for real-time adjustments based on campaign performance data.
8. Personalization: It enables businesses to craft relevant, personalized messages that resonate with potential buyers at different stages of the customer journey.

Digital marketers are responsible for managing online campaigns, crafting and executing digital strategies, monitoring campaign performance, engaging with audiences across social media platforms, and collaborating with content creators and designers to deliver cohesive campaigns.

To illustrate this progression, consider how Dollar Shave Club combined digital marketing with influencer partnerships. Their viral 2012 YouTube ad, featuring the CEO, leveraged micro-influencers to target niche audiences – a strategy that blended content marketing and social media outreach.

The success of digital marketing campaigns often relies on creativity, emotional storytelling, and leveraging user-generated content. Campaigns like Apple's #ShotOniPhone and Airbnb's 'Made Possible by Hosts' demonstrate how effective digital marketing can build emotional connections, inspire action, and drive long-term business growth.

Because we would like to have a comprehensive perspective of digital marketing landscape, it is time to present the influencer marketing concept. Influencer marketing is a form of social media marketing that leverages the popularity and credibility of individuals who have a dedicated and engaged following on platforms like Instagram, YouTube, TikTok, and Twitter/X. These influencers, who can range from celebrities to niche content creators, collaborate with brands to promote products or services to their audience. The effectiveness of influencer marketing lies in its ability to tap into established communities and utilize the trust and rapport that influencers have built with their followers.

To implement an influencer marketing campaign, brands typically start by identifying influencers whose audience aligns with their target demographic. They then reach out to these influencers, often through agencies or platforms specializing in influencer collaborations, to negotiate partnerships. These partnerships can take various forms, including sponsored posts, product reviews, brand ambassadorships, or co-created content. The key to successful influencer marketing is ensuring authenticity and alignment between the influencer's personal brand and the product being promoted.

The cost of influencer marketing can vary widely, depending on factors such as the influencer's reach, engagement rates, and the scope of the campaign. Micro-influencers (typically with 10,000 to 100,000 followers) might charge anywhere from €100 to €500 per post, while macro-influencers or celebrities can command tens of thousands of euros for a single collaboration. Influencer marketing is particularly worth the investment when targeting younger demographics, launching new products, or entering markets where traditional advertising may be less effective. It's especially valuable for brands looking to build authenticity and trust, as influencers can provide a more personal and relatable endorsement compared to traditional advertising methods. There should be a personalized assessment for the company planning to use influencer marketing; such assessment includes a variety of criteria, the most important one being the cost-benefit.

Personal branding consists of the communication of personal values to the world and the position one might get in customers' minds. Simply put, the perceptions people have about you. As the entrepreneur, at least in the early stages, you are the interface and image of your enterprise/organization. You can't detach your personal branding from your start-up because the company comes with your values, purpose, and vision. Building your personal brand takes time and effort and should be done consistently through a well-designed strategy to gain the maximum visibility (personal branding strategy).

A personal brand statement is a brief and summarized content mostly in one sentence. For example:

> Empowering ridiculously good marketing.
>
> (Ann Handley)

> Real life on a budget.
>
> (Jessi Fearon)

> Practical Help for Freelance Writers.
>
> (Carol Tice)

> Travel smarter, cheaper, longer. Where do you want to go?
>
> (Matthew Kepnes, @nomadicmatt)

and so on.

So, now is time to reflect. Please write down a few sentences that would characterize you or are representative for you and what you would like to offer in terms of business. Do not worry about perfection; write everything down. You will have time to polish and rewrite them later.

1. ______________________________
2. ______________________________
3. ______________________________

4. ________________________
5. ________________________
6. ________________________
7. ________________________

Market size (or market potential, also called total available market or TAM) is a term that refers to the total number of potential customers that a company can serve.

Served available market (SAM) represents the subset of TAM accessible through your current distribution channels (e.g., residents within delivery radius for a restaurant).

The target market (also called serviceable obtainable market or SOM) represents the market segment one can get based on the current business practices or business model.

Let's take the example of a restaurant to identify the real market segment. In this case, the market would be:

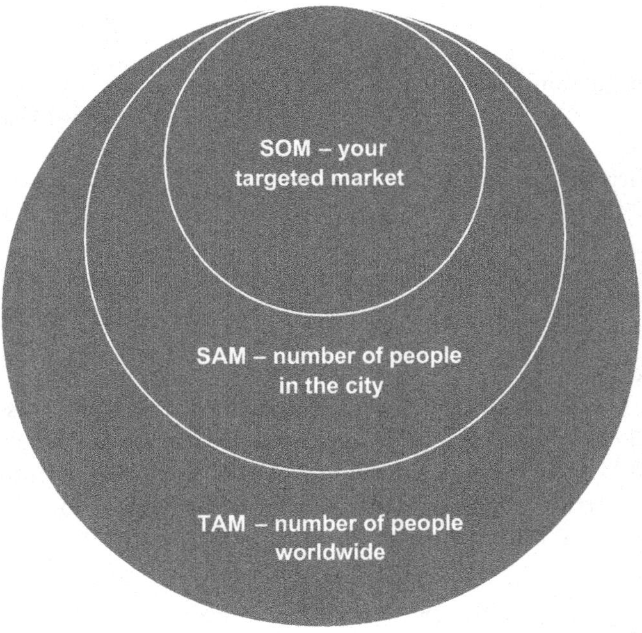

Figure 7.1 General market categories.

SOM – the real targeted market that you will attract in reality are those living nearby or employees of a company with HQs or working facilities next to you (for the obvious reasons). Realistically speaking, your marketing efforts in this case should concentrate exclusively on this segment.

Meanwhile, if you have an e-commerce website selling non-food items, then the situation changes; due to huge technological progress, transportation, logistics, and payment processors, anyone in the world could order from your website, and you can ship the product to their location. If it is about digital products or services, the situation is even easier, as everything can be delivered online: a download link or a teleconsultation through specific software.

Market share is defined as the segment or section of the market controlled by a company or by a product or service. There are few formulas to calculate this, but the most frequent one is:

(Company total sales/Market total sales) × *100* = *% of market captured or market share*

The next question would be how someone can find the total market sales or any similar data. There are several resources for this: the national institute for statistics in your country, national bank, ministry of commerce, World Trade Organization, OECD, regional statistics (for example, EUROSTAT in Europe), some industry interests' groups, large consulting firms' reports, and so on.

As a company, you can have a model of B2B (business-to-business) or B2C (business-to-consumers) business. The B2B model means that you, as a company, have only other businesses as customers. In this case, you know the customers by name (the company, the person you are doing business with, the owner, people in the department you are dealing with, etc.), and your marketing strategy is different from the one for B2C. In B2B cases, companies are searching for suppliers who can provide not only a product but also knowledge/information and market insights and have the potential to become long-terms strategic partners.

The B2C model means that you serve the final users or the consumers. A supermarket or your neighborhood shop is an example of

B2C business. In this case, you know your customers or customers through their purchasing patterns, purchasing power, income levels, gender, or other identifiers relevant to you as a business for marketing purposes.

Going back to the consumers, it is relevant to discuss Rogers' diffusion of innovation concepts. E.M. Rogers developed innovation diffusion theory in 1962, aiming to explain how product/services or ideas diffuse over time through a specific social system (or population). Adopting a new product/service or idea means that a person behaves in a different way than in the past. The main element of adoption is that the person must perceive the new idea beneficial to them, fitting their values or belief systems, and even contributing to improvements. From the following graph, we can see five categories of customers. These categories are:

1. *The innovators* who are dedicated to being among the first to try innovative products and services; new ideas appeal to such people. You just need to make them aware of the innovation for them to try it.
2. *Early adopters* include opinion leaders. This category embraces change and enjoys leading people. They also spread the word and encourage further adoptions. To this segment, information worksheets and guiding manuals are appealing.
3. *Early majority* includes people who need to see evidence and testimonials about the efficiency of the innovation before adopting it.
4. *Late majority* includes people who are reluctant to change and adopt something new if they do not see results on a large scale.
5. *Late adopters* (or laggards) are the very conservative category and change-averse people. To convince this section of the population, one needs hard evidence, pressure from other groups, and fear appeals.

In the following, you can see a graph of these categories of innovation adopters or customer. As shown in Figure 7.2, Rogers' innovation adoption curve segments customers into five distinct groups, from tech-forward innovators to skeptical laggards.

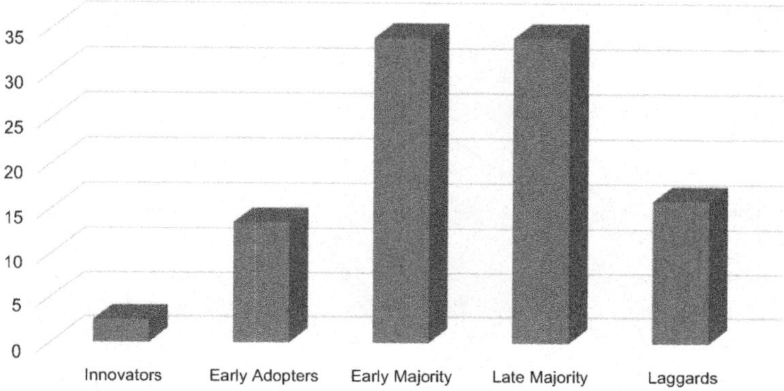

Figure 7.2 Rogers' diffusion of innovation theory.[1]

The next important concept to understand and make use of is the product life cycle (PLC) concept. PLC is a critical concept in marketing that outlines the stages a product goes through from its introduction to its eventual decline. Each stage presents unique opportunities and challenges, requiring tailored marketing strategies to maximize profitability and market relevance.

The PLC has four phases: introduction of the product on the market, growth stage, maturity stage, and decline (the exit from the market of a product). Let's have a look at each one.

1. **Introduction phase**: when the product is launched into the market. Sales are typically low, as customers are not yet familiar with the product, and businesses face high costs due to development, promotion, and distribution.

   Marketing strategies suitable for products in this phase:

   - **Product**: Focus on building awareness by highlighting the product's unique value proposition.
   - **Price**: Use penetration pricing (low prices to attract customers) or skimming pricing (high prices to recover development costs).
   - **Promotion**: Heavy investment in advertising to educate potential customers.

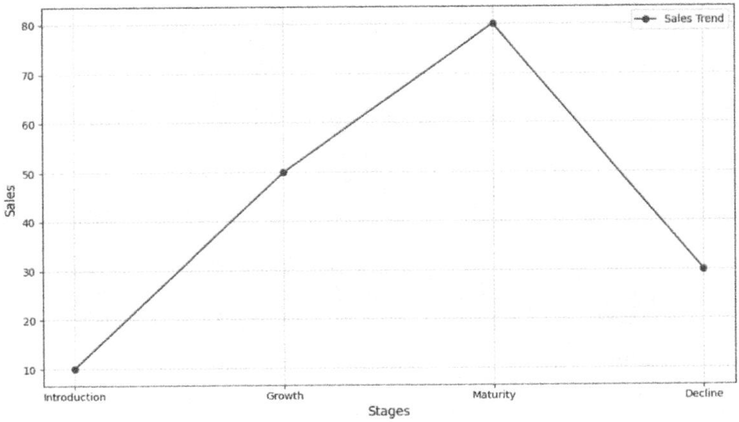

Figure 7.3 Product life cycle.

- **Distribution**: Selective distribution to ensure availability in key markets.

Let's have a look at Tesla's launch of its electric vehicles (EVs); it involved extensive marketing campaigns to educate consumers about EV benefits while using premium pricing to emphasize innovation.

2. **Growth phase**: demand increases as customers become aware of the product. Sales grow rapidly, and competitors may enter the market.

   Marketing strategies suitable for products in this phase:

- **Product**: Enhance features based on customer feedback.
- **Price**: Maintain competitive pricing while maximizing profit margins.
- **Promotion**: Broaden marketing efforts to target a larger audience.
- **Distribution**: Expand distribution channels to meet growing demand.

A good example for this phase is Apple's iPhone. During its growth phase, it focused on expanding its global reach while introducing new features like App Store integration, which differentiated it from competitors.

3. **Maturity phase**: the product reaches peak sales during this stage, but growth slows as the market becomes saturated. Competition intensifies, and companies must focus on differentiation. Marketing strategies suitable for products in this phase:

   - **Product**: Introduce variations or upgrades (e.g., new colors or improved models).
   - **Price**: Use competitive pricing to retain market share.
   - **Promotion**: Shift focus toward customer loyalty programs and targeted campaigns.
   - **Distribution**: Optimize channels with incentives for retailers.

   The best possible example for this phase is Coca-Cola and its products. Coca Cola has maintained its maturity phase by innovating with new flavors, packaging designs, and personalized marketing campaigns (especially before traditional celebrations) while keeping prices competitive.

4. **Decline phase**: sales decline as consumer interest wanes due to market saturation or newer alternatives. Companies must decide whether to rejuvenate or phase out the product. Marketing strategies suitable for products in this phase:

   - **Product**: Simplify offerings or find niche uses for the product.
   - **Price**: Reduce prices to clear inventory or sustain niche demand.
   - **Promotion**: Minimize spending but focus on targeted promotions.
   - **Distribution**: Limit distribution to profitable markets (if any).

The best example for this phase is the DVD players. DVD players experienced a severe decline with the rise of streaming services like Netflix. Companies reduced production and focused on niche markets like educational institutions still using DVDs.

The product life cycle is a powerful framework that helps businesses adapt their marketing strategies at each stage of a product's journey. By understanding customer needs and market dynamics at every phase – introduction, growth, maturity, and decline – companies can maximize profitability and extend their products' relevance in competitive markets. Applying these strategies effectively ensures sustainable success across diverse industries.

Some common sales techniques you might hear often are the following:

FOMO, or fear of missing out, is a term you might hear or see used frequently. The most common approach is pressuring you to buy until a certain date; otherwise, you will be losing some bonuses or the price will increase significantly (such as early bid or a workshop with special offers), or you might not have another chance to buy.

FOBO, or fear of missing out on better opportunities, means that you might not be convinced that a specific offer is the best one in terms of price or conditions. So, one might not buy or might postpone a purchase because one would like to search for better options.

Marketing channels[2] are all the channels (the complete link) through which products/services move from the manufacturing place to the final consumer. It is a holistic chain made from people, companies, activities, and processes dedicated to transfer of the product to the customer. Any market channel can be part of the sales funnel you crafted for your company.

A sales funnel is a graphic representation representing the customer journey from being aware of you and your product until purchase is realized. There are automation marketing and sales tools that can help in this regard,[3] and in the era of digitalization and the Internet of Things (IoT), it has become a kind of necessity. The sales funnel has four stages, usually known by the AIDA acronym. In this case, AIDA stands for *awareness*, *interest*, *decision*, and *action*.

AIDA FRAMEWORK EXPLAINED

Awareness represents the moment when a potential customer becomes aware of your brand, product, or company. This can happen in any way, from word of mouth to a shared post on social

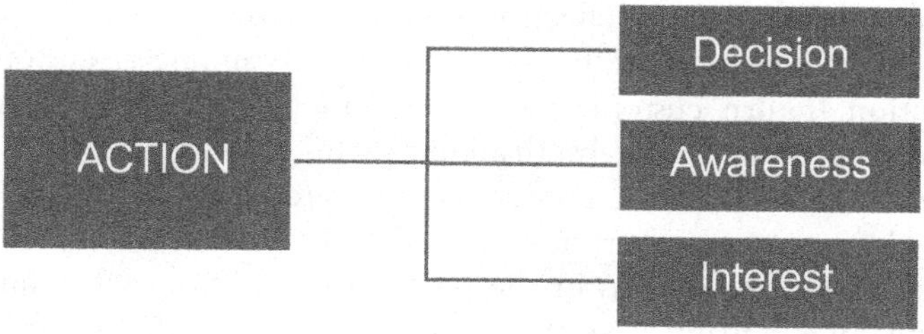

Figure 7.4 AIDA framework graphic representation.

Note: The action phase represents the lead conversion rate, meaning the number of customers who are really buying in the end. As a business, the aim is to increase the rate as much as possible and increase purchases among our 'acquired' customers.

media or paid advertisements via Google ads. Aggressive pushing is *not* a viable option; this will only scare away the potential customers or cause people to unsubscribe from your social media campaigns.

Interest is the phase where you establish your specialty or expertise and help the potential customer to make an informed decision. The potential customer is in the exploring phase, comparing options and discussing the alternatives with family or friends, or just taking some time to think it over. In this phase, you can inform the potential customer about the advantages of buying from you, the situation in which a product or service is useful or recommended, and testimonials or evidence available. If you wish to capture the email of the visitor, then you should offer something of value in exchange; this value could be a discount code, a book of interest, something free, free delivery for the next order, or a mix of several bonuses.

Decision is the phase where a potential customer makes the purchasing decision and has to choose between two or three options. This is the perfect time to give a special offer or discount, free shipping, or anything additional to make the offer more attractive. If you have a landing page, there are several add-ons that monitor where a potential customer stopped reading; other add-ons offer the opportunity to track when a customer wants to close the page and then launch a special offer to convince the potential customer to read on and hopefully make the purchase.

Action is the phase of effective purchasing. Your duty as the provider does not end here because you are also aiming at customer retention (return customers). So you should connect with your customers after the sale by thanking them, encouraging them to provide feedback on the product/service/processes, and specifying how they can get support in case they might need it.

Measuring the success or the performance of your sales funnel can be done in many ways; the most common one is the conversion rate. Conversion rate can be the number of people subscribing to your updates or newsletter from the social media campaigns or the number of people actually buying the product as a result of your social media or Google Ads campaign.

The next obvious question is, 'How can someone implement this into their future business?' This can be done in a few easy steps; I do recommend using an automation tool because it can help in measuring the performance of your campaigns as well.

Step 1: Understanding your customer – as discussed, by now, you should have segmented your market and have a customer avatar. Keep in mind that your marketing campaigns are for those in need of your product or service.

Step 2: Capture attention – through targeted marketing and sales campaigns. One organic way to grow is engaging your audience by posting regularly on your social media and offering valuable content via your newsletters.

Step 3: Your landing page – where you offer detailed info about you, your product, and service, and you instruct the potential customer on what to do next. For example, 'Press the red button below for a live demo or to get a special discount available in the next 30 minutes' (in combination with FOMO).

Step 4: Your email campaigns – should not be very aggressive or too frequent; readers expect valuable content not to unsubscribe. Remember, the focus must be on customers and their needs. A no at this moment is not a permanent no. The approach should be this: get in touch, find out the reason behind the negative response, keep in touch, and approach the person again in a few months with a customized business proposal. It is highly recommended to do your homework and find out everything possible about your potential business partners.

Step 5: Stay in touch with your customers – as well as potential customers. Customers need to feel that they matter and are heard. You should address all the positive and negative reviews in a constructive manner.

It is important to remember that the focus of sales must be the customer and the need. It is essential to communicate that when you approach the customer. Instead of saying, 'I have this website where you can add your cars for sale,' you should say, 'Would you like to increase your sales by 10% in the next 6 months?' Please note that whatever you sell must be realistic, and you must be able to deliver on your promise. The customer expects value in return for money and for delivering what was promised.

Objections are an inevitable component of the sale process (most sales come with objections from customers for various reasons). As I like to say, the objections come in many shapes and forms. Each objection is a lesson to be learnt and to be prepared for in the future. It is very important to list the value you offer, benefits of using your product or service, guarantees, and evidence, as well as to address the most common objections (such as price, utility, post-sale support, and life cycle) clearly on your website or landing page. The most common objection one can meet is about price: Either it is too expensive, the customer can't afford it now or does not have money now, or there is another money-related issue. So, how can you address such objections?

First, you need to open a conversation and understand the customer's comparison or the real issue behind the objection – either the customer would like to search alternatives and compare prices or does not have all the money to pay upfront, and so on. This will offer you the opportunity to discuss the value you provide and alternatives, the customer's budget, and competitors with the prospective customer.[4] You can continue the discussion and reach the cost of opportunity talk, meaning reminding the prospective customer what they are missing if they do not act.[5]

Customers are essentials for business survival. Each business aims to retain the current customers and, ideally, gain new ones. Retaining current customers is cheaper than gaining new ones. Keeping customers happy, getting feedback, and constantly measuring their level of satisfaction with the product or service we deliver is vital for business success and survival.

At first glance, customer perception appears to be an easy idea; it refers to a consumer's overall impression of a business at any given time during their interaction with the brand. What is more difficult is identifying and quantifying the numerous factors that shape the experience of the client. Fortunately, providing high-quality customer service is a direct path to enhancing customers' opinions of a business. The reason for this is that customer service affects consumer perception through contentment numbers.

For a company's success, its image in the eyes of its clientele is crucial. Successful brand management occurs when a company can convince consumers to pay more for a product that is essentially identical to others in the market.

Using a *customer-centric approach* is extremely valuable nowadays as the post-pandemic shift in customers' purchasing behavior is even more visible. Measuring customer perceptions and introducing marketing efforts for managing them are both part of the customer-centric marketing approach. This includes all the activities and campaigns of the company to be focused on the needs and perceptions of the customers. Likert scales are usually used in this type of marketing, as they can help the company gain a better insight into the customers.

Client-centric approach can be put into practice by ensuring and prioritizing customer empathy. The brands need to communicate how the company cares about the need of the customers. Moreover, customers must have a personalized experience, for which the company needs to understand the customer profiles and their purchase histories.

A *Likert scale*, which is also known as a scoring system, is a statistical tool that is utilized in research investigations to evaluate respondents' ideas, perspectives, and/or emotions. Subjects are given a selection of possible answers to choose from in response to each statement or inquiry. Likert scales can be used to evaluate aspects such as frequency, quality, or a person's feelings regarding the significance of a particular characteristic. For instance, you could make use of a Likert scale to learn how customers feel about specific product features or which product updates they would most want to see next based on a selection of available choices.

When quantitative data is being collected, the scale can be an extremely flexible tool to use. You will be able to see levels of judgment, which will offer you a more precise and representative view of the information that you get as a result of the precision that the scale provides compared to basic yes or no answers.

There are several things that should be taken into consideration when drafting questions to be answered using a Likert scale to guarantee that correct replies are obtained and that respondents understand what is being asked of them. It is important that all data collected be anonymous and comply with the General Data Protection Regulation (GDPR).

- *Don't overcomplicate things* – Asking direct and uncomplicated questions is the most effective method for obtaining precise results. Make it absolutely clear what you want the respondents to evaluate, whether it is their preferences, their opinions, or something else entirely.
- *Ensure that the scales are consistent with one another* – It is important for respondents to have a thorough understanding of the scale against which they will be requested to record their responses; doing so will ensure that their responses on either side of the scale are consistent. Providing enough explanations of the questions and answers' rating is mandatory.
- *Avoid making claims; seek information* – Instead of making statements, you should ask questions when developing an effective Likert scale. By doing things this way, you eliminate the possibility of prejudice and give respondents the chance to answer. The rationale for this is that individuals tend to instinctively agree with assertions that are favorable or established or behave in a positive way when they are presented with positive statements. In the big picture, this can cast doubt on the reliability of your study.

In addition, when statements are avoided in preference of questions, participants are forced to give answers that are less influenced by prejudice since they must first consider their options.

A great example for managing customer perceptions is Snickers. What factors influence a person's decision to take a Snickers bar instead of any other chocolate when they are faced with a choice between hundreds of chocolate-covered bars? Yes, it could be a matter of taste or preference, but the company has devised ingenious marketing efforts to convince consumers that eating a Snickers bar will turn them from irritable and distracted to alert and content. The marketing efforts are fruitful and made the customers satisfied with the product.

Let's have a look at a simple scale for measuring customers' perception. These questions can be adapted, expanded, or modified so they can serve your company's specific purpose for getting customers' feedback.

This type of Likert scale can help ensure that the company's marketing efforts are changing the customer's perception for good. Referring to the Snickers example, marketing efforts are completely based on the customer's perception and attitude toward the chocolate and the previous measured impact.

The company started a new marketing campaign recently to change the customers' perceptions about the brand. It started depicting the Snickers bar as the ultimate solution to hunger regardless of where the consumers are. The brand adopted a client-centric marketing technique, targeting customers when they were most hungry by sending coupons to their smartphones. This demonstrates how a client-centric approach can help to transform how consumers perceive the business and its products.

The next important tool in assessing customers' experience is the *customer journey map*. A customer's interaction with a company can be represented graphically using a customer journey map. This

Table 7.1 Simple scale for measuring perception (example)

Question	1	2	3	4	5
How satisfied are you with the product's taste?					
How satisfied are you with the product's packaging?					
How satisfied are you with the price?					

Scale explanation: On the scale, 1 = very unsatisfied, 2 = dissatisfied, 3 = neither unsatisfied nor satisfied, 4 = satisfied, and 5 = very satisfied with the product or service.

depicts the path a customer follows as they interact with a company on a variety of levels. A customer journey map must consider not only the interactions and events of truth but also the feelings (such as discontent or doubt) and intended actions (such as transactions) of your core demographic.

Data-driven customer journey maps enable you to comprehend the tasks that the consumers need to complete when interacting with a site or product, in addition to what they are considering and experiencing at each stage of their experience. When you gather insightful information, you can delve deeper into how consumers connect with your business, which makes it simpler for you to connect with what they are going through. If you have a solid grasp of the user's demands across all their contacts, you will be able to see any loopholes in the experience and either add new connections or improve the ones that already exist.

Awareness – At the very peak of the purchaser's pipeline is the stage known as 'awareness,' which represents the very first step in the buying process. The consumer understands that they have an issue or demand, and they are ready to do something about it.

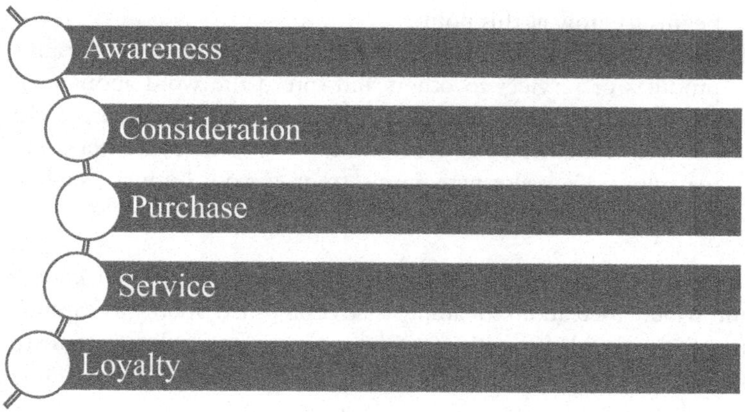

Figure 7.5 Graphic representation of customer journey experience.

Note: It is important to know each segment of the customers' experience well so that one can find out where to intervene. Nowadays, there are marketing tracking apps that measure the customers' engagement for each stage.

The consumer will begin with broad research. At the start of the awareness stage, the buyer is not yet prepared to make a purchase. However, the shopper's true goal is only to get inspiration. Making the buyer aware of your items is more important at this point than actually closing a deal.

Consideration – The moment the consumer understands that there is a void to satisfy or a challenge to overcome, they will begin the process of weighing their available choices. The consideration phase is where a customer begins to really think about making a purchase. A key goal at this point in the customer experience ought to be to ignite the client's desire to investigate the prospect of utilizing your products or services.

Purchase – If the sales and advertising efforts were fruitful, you will continue onto the acquisition phase. At this point, you should do everything you can to help your buyer complete the transaction. Assist them in making the switch and setting up the new equipment to make the transaction as painless as possible.

Service – The following stage is the support that is delivered to the customers for boosting their loyalty and enhancing the encounter even after the transaction is done. With the support of the company's after-sale services, the customer's loyalty to the brand begins to grow at this point.

Loyalty – Satisfied customers are more likely to promote a company's products or services to others and spread the word about your business. Now, all that's left to do is keep providing excellent service. Nonetheless, if you want to wow your consumers, you may always seek alternative ways to grow your business, such as introducing brand-new products or services.

How does this apply in practice? One of the most well-known and widely used audio streaming services is called Spotify. As Spotify sought to provide its users with a better experience when it came to sharing music, the company contracted the services of a marketing consultancy to develop a customer journey map. This mapping of the customer journey was created to determine where music sharing capabilities would be most beneficial in the customer experience. Spotify's 2019 'Wrapped' campaign used customer journey mapping to transform raw streaming data into personalized year-end summaries. This strategy increased social shares by 21% by aligning with users' desire for self-expression during the loyalty stage.

During each step, the company outlines what a consumer is involved with, what they're performing, what they are thinking about, and how they are feeling. This is the stage where data for raising awareness was collected by the company. This data was extracted by the company using data analysis and customer feedback to gain a better understanding of how consumers felt at each stage of the customer experience. Customers are suggested music based on the information collected, taking them to the consideration stage. After the customers have made the decision and subscribed to the app, this is where the purchase happens.

The after-sale service is ensured by the company through its website, call center, and mainly FAQs section to increase customer loyalty.

It is important for any company not to forget about the existing customers or past customers. Loyalty programs, discounts and keeping in touch with them through a variety of communication channels and engage with past and present customers.

Marketing is not just about selling – it's about solving, connecting, and evolving. Whether you're calculating TAM for a neighborhood café or designing a Spotify-worthy customer journey, remember: every data point, every ad campaign, and every post-purchase survey is a chance to refine your story. The digital age hasn't changed the fundamentals; it's given us sharper tools to listen, adapt, and innovate. So go beyond the funnel. Be the brand that doesn't just meet expectations but reshapes them – one authentic interaction, one strategic insight, and one customer-first decision at a time. Your market isn't out there waiting; it's yours to create.

NOTES

1 Adapted from Rogers, E. M. (1962). *Diffusion of Innovations*. New York: Free Press.

2 If you are unsure and you decide to cooperate with a specialist to make an informed decision, ask them about their results. In the end, you are paying them to get results in terms of number of visits, conversion rate (the % of people who are buying from the total visits), or new followers on social media and organic growth, quality content, and so on. Again, establish SMART objectives with quantitative measurable results as you decide and agree with the provider.

3 Some tools that can be tested and considered for such a purpose are Salesforce, Campaigner, Getresponse, Infusionsoft, and so on.
4 Knowing your competition and their prices and offers is a must. Knowing what you offer and how you differentiate yourself from the rest is among the essential information that should be conveyed as often as possible.
5 Remember: Each sale is about the customer, their needs, and the perceived value of what you are offering to them. This subject is treated in detail in the next chapter.

8

DIGITAL EMPATHY IN ACTION

Resolving complaints, building trust, and winning online

Responding in a professional way to customers' feedback, either positive or negative, is an important component of marketing. Nowadays, a lot of such feedback is expressed via social media.

Negative feedback is inevitable. Even the best companies have unhappy consumers. Any customer feedback can help your business for future improvements and developments. Addressing customer issues is one of the best ways to handle unfavorable online reviews.

Criticism and negative feedback are not easy to manage because they can sometimes be perceived as personal, offensive, and unrealistic. The customer's negative feedback can be handled in the following ways:

1. *Take a deep breath and stay calm*
   Negative reviews may be demoralizing. Not to worry. Unsatisfied customers didn't obtain the promised outcomes or benefits, which are not always your fault. Keep calm and seek the truth. Practically, try to focus on the reasons for receiving criticism and understand what is acceptable for the customer as resolution.
2. *Personalize your response*
   First, let's empathize by using the name of the customer (humanization). Show the customer that you care beyond giving a response. To be seen and heard is fundamental for customers, and businesses need to be keen on this. Those who've had negative feedback will appreciate this because it will show you how to be prepared better

DOI: 10.4324/9781003591429-9

in the future and address the complaints either through better communication or product or service improvement.

3. *Thank them for their feedback*
   Always be grateful for feedback, favorable or bad. You owe it to the person who shared their experience to learn from it, understand the causes/reasons for the negative feedback, and make better decisions in the future.
4. *Apologize and show empathy*
   Empathy is an excellent beginning step in addressing unhappy customers' complaints and difficulties. Don't blame others for your faults; apologize instead. Let them know you understand their complaint or negative response.
5. *Focus*
   Don't ignore consumers' issues. Focus on the problem and feedback. Don't change the subject to divert consumers' rage.
6. *Request another chance*
   An apology without action is useless. Agree with the customer for compensation; this could be a product replacement, reimbursement, or future discounts. Consult your team and find ways to improve what went wrong.

Let's have a look at some hypothetical situations and potential response.

COMPLAINT REGARDING DISSATISFACTION WITH A MEAL

COMPLAINT

'Today I ordered a salad that had falafel in it. Tiny and tasteless, the falafel came with a side of dry lettuce. It was inedible to me.'

POTENTIAL RESPONSE

'Hi there, [Customer Name]
I appreciate you taking the time to provide us with the feedback. We sincerely apologize for the inconvenience created. We understand that you have certain expectations while ordering from our restaurant.

We're deeply sorry your meal didn't meet expectations. Fresh ingredients are our priority, and we'll investigate this lapse immediately. To make it right, we'd like to offer a complimentary replacement meal and a 20% discount on your next order (code: FRESH20). Please reply to this message or call us at [phone number] to arrange this.

Thank you for your understanding.

The manager'

COMPLAINT ABOUT THE APP NOT WORKING

COMPLAINT

'I have been trying to open the banking application for hours, but it is not working.'

POTENTIAL RESPONSE

'Dear [Customer Name], we are sorry to learn about you having an issue with the application. Please note that your complaint has been forwarded to the technical team on an urgent basis. Our technical team is prioritizing your case and will resolve this within 2 hours. We'll send a confirmation SMS once fixed and a $10 credit for the inconvenience.

We would like to apologize for any inconvenience.

The manager'

As a company, you can create some norms to assist you with responding to customers' complaint. Formulate a plan for responding to customer concerns and work hard to resolve them in a timely, equitable, and effective way.

Furthermore, the plan needs to:

1. Provide specific instructions on the official complaint process.
2. Detail the process you'll follow to hear, analyze, and settle customer concerns.
3. Provide examples of how you may address customer concerns.
4. Show your consumers that you're dedicated to improving every day.

After settling on a policy, a process for dealing with complaints may be drafted. Having a set protocol in place will make sure that complaints are always handled in the same manner. All your employees should be able to pick up on the method without any trouble.

Some possible stages in your method are as follows.

- Listen to the complaint carefully and with empathy
  You should express gratitude to the customer for alerting you on the problem. Make amends, take responsibility, avoid shifting blame, and be polite. Ensure that the customer has visibility of how the problem will be taken care of. Take notes and ask questions until you are clear about all the aspects of the situation.
- Note the details of the feedback.
  Read the complaint carefully to make sure you grasp the issue at hand. Don't lose track of the many complaints that have been filed. This can be made easier by keeping a proper record of the complaints received and a structured policy to resolve them or transfer them to appropriate departments. Centralize the complaints and identify the frequent issues appearing in those complaints.
- Focus on all the facts
  Verify that you fully understand and document the nature of the complaint. If you have any doubts, just ask the customer. Create a proper communication channel, such as email or a phone call. This can also help the customer feel better about the brand and be convinced that whatever problem they might have will be properly taken care of.
- Discuss the remedy for the issue
  Whether it's a fix, a replacement, a refund, or an apology, you should ask the consumer what they're hoping to hear back from you about. Consider how practical it would be to grant this wish. You might even establish a plan that will allow for only certain actions to be taken in such situations.
- Take quick action
  Get the problem fixed as soon as possible. When delays occur, problems often get worse. This is done by mainly focusing, keeping the problems you received first as your priority. It is important to set a timeframe for complaints resolution and inform the customer from the beginning.
- Fulfill your commitment
  If there are any holdups in addressing the customer's request, be sure to keep them updated. Don't make promises you can't keep.

- Follow up with the customer
  Get in touch with the customer and find out whether they are pleased with the outcome of their complaint.

For example, if a customer has complained about receiving a faulty product, the company should be listening to the complaint carefully without placing the blame on the customer for having destroyed the product. This should be followed by ensuring that the product received by the customer is replaced and quick action is taken. Moreover, once the customer has received the replacement, the company should follow up and ensure that the product is intact and that the customer is satisfied.

A complaint resolution workflow within a company can be as follows:

1. Receiving the complaint: customer submits feedback via email, social media, or phone.
2. Acknowledge and empathize: respond within few hours or as soon as possible (e.g., '*Hi [Name], thank you for alerting us . . .*') and apologize sincerely ('*We're deeply sorry . . .*').
3. Investigate: log details in a centralized system (product/service, date, issue specifics) and assign it to a relevant team/person (e.g., technical, kitchen, logistics).
4. Resolve as soon as possible: if there is an issue with a product, offer a replacement; if there is a problem with the service, either offer a refund or credit for future purchases.
5. Follow-up: confirm the resolution via email/call ('*Is everything resolved to your satisfaction?*') and invite additional feedback (e.g., post-resolution survey).
6. Analyze complaint issues: Use complaint logs to identify recurring issues (e.g., dry lettuce, app crashes) and share the findings with the concerned teams for systemic improvements.

Nowadays, more than ever before, we have almost fully digitized systems. Customers and companies are doing their best to use it for their full benefits and potential. In today's digital era, companies of all sizes may benefit from social media marketing. Effective social media marketing can do wonders for a company, from attracting new customers to inspiring existing ones to talk about their products.

The following recommendations are meant to assist interested parties in obtaining benefits and revenue through social media:

1. *Use the social network your followers are on*
   You need to locate the social media platforms where your potential customers hang out online and take advantage of those platforms as well. Instagram is a highly used platform for such purpose; LinkedIn is more for professionals, while Facebook still sees wide usage.
2. *The content you are posting must be excellent*
   It may seem like an easy principle for digital marketers to put quality ahead of quantity, yet many still make this mistake. You won't see the levels of participation you want if your material is only adequate.
3. *Facilitate purchases through social media*
   Companies may categorize their inventory or e-commerce platform according to the attributes of the actual goods they sell. You can engage with your community or customers, redirect them to landing pages to read about the offer and complete a purchase, or inform them about different advantages of your product or service.
4. *Instagram (Snapchat, TikTok, Twitter, etc.) as a lead-generation tool*
   Gaining followers on Instagram is excellent, but turning them into customers is even better. Making your feed postings more engaging is a terrific strategy for attracting more subscribers.
5. *Promote your company on LinkedIn to reach more people*
   Through LinkedIn's groups, programmatic display ads, and sponsored InMail, among other channels, your company may network with other businesses, get new prospects, and raise brand recognition.
6. *Advertisements that cost money*
   To boost sales, you need more than just active social media profiles and prompt responses to comments. Paid advertisements are the best method for maximizing the potential of your social media profiles. Allocate 20% of budgets to retargeting cart abandoners.
7. *Crisis management*
   Monitor sentiment daily with Hootsuite; respond publicly within few hours to feedback, reviews, complaints, requests, and so on.

To sell your products or services, you need a strategy. Funnel marketing is such a strategy, and it entails sending communications to customers at every point in the buying process. It considers the whole 360-degree customer journey, trying to strengthen connections and enhance brand experiences rather than just increasing revenue.

The best full-funnel approaches are data driven. By compiling information from many internal and external sources, you may better target your efforts and get optimal results at every turn of the trip. Consequently, sales increase, and return on investment rises.

Phases of the funnel strategy are:

- *Awareness* – Potential customers have problems but aren't yet familiar with your company or product. The goal is to attract prospective consumers by providing material that is interesting, helpful, and simple to find. For example, a company can run advertisements on Instagram to ensure higher customer reach and spread the message widely.
- *Interest* – You've got their attention now, and they're looking for, or at least curious about, the information that will assist them with their issue. The goal is to have customers think of you rather than the competitors when they need your products or services, and this is accomplished by gaining their trust and maintaining their interest via consistently useful marketing communications. For example, the company can post online reviews from other consumers.
- *Appraisal* – In this stage, customers are searching for the best alternative that meets their need and budget. They are searching for the company that can offer the best value for the budget they have. For this purpose, you should inform your potential customers about promotions or offers you might have, benefits they can get, or additional post-sale services through newsletters, digital freebies, how-to manuals, and interesting videos.
- *Conversion* – At this point, prospects have developed an understanding of your brand and are responsive to your brand messaging. While considering the marketing funnel as a whole, it is important to use a broad net to draw in prospective customers at the very top of the funnel. It is important at this stage to ease the conversion process and make the purchase smooth for the customer. For this purpose, the company can introduce a help

desk or FAQ section to make it easier for the customers to order and read all about the products beforehand.
- *Loyalty* – A common mistake made by many companies is to assume that after their main conversion objective has been reached, the marketing funnel is complete. However, the customer's journey and the return on investment from your efforts to reach that conversion objective are only getting started. For example, the company can retain loyalty by offering repeated customers some discount and promos.
- *Advocacy or referral programs* – Users are those that go out of their way to suggest your business to others. In this step, the company can introduce referral promos to ensure more audience, an increased number of customers, and possible retention of the current customers.

Let's have a look at Amazon as a very good example of the funnel strategy. Amazon Prime employs a data-driven approach to guide customers through the purchasing journey. It begins with *awareness campaigns* on YouTube and Instagram, where ads emphasize fast delivery to attract time-conscious shoppers. Once interest is piqued, personalized emails highlight trending products aligned with individual browsing histories, nurturing consideration. At the *conversion stage*, one-click checkout and free returns minimize friction, simplifying purchases. To foster *loyalty*, Prime members gain exclusive access to deals and streaming content, enhancing long-term satisfaction. Finally, the 'Invite Friends' referral program incentivizes *advocacy*, rewarding users for expanding Prime's subscriber base while reinforcing brand loyalty through shared benefits. This end-to-end strategy exemplifies how seamless integration of funnel stages can amplify customer retention and growth.

Another example can be of an online e-commerce business of cosmetic products. The company knows the target customers well, as they are women from 20 to 45 years of age. If the majority of these women use Facebook or Instagram, the company will start running advertisements to create awareness among the customers. When they see the ads, they start considering the products and website and start exploring them. The website here should be user friendly to help the process reach the step of conversion where women buy the products. There can be many offers, such as free delivery, to encourage this step. Loyalty rewards or points can help the company retain customers, whereas good customer service can cause the customer to advocate for the company.

Every complaint is a hidden blueprint for growth – a chance to transform frustration into loyalty and criticism into innovation. By embracing these moments with empathy, urgency, and systemic rigor, you're not just resolving issues but building unshakable trust. Remember: the most resilient businesses aren't those that avoid missteps but those that turn setbacks into stepping stones. Let every interaction reinforce this truth: your commitment to excellence isn't defined by perfection but by how you rise, refine, and relentlessly improve. Now go – turn detractors into advocates, and watch loyalty becomes your most powerful currency.

9

FRANCHISING + DESIGN THINKING

The blueprint for risk-proof innovation

Franchising refers to the acquisition of rights to sell goods or services under a specific brand; as part of the contract, the franchisee also needs to comply with franchisor's requirements in terms of royalty, entry fee, trainings, location, raw materials, and other terms.

Some of the most famous franchises are McDonalds, Burger King, Starbucks, Marriott International, Subway, RE/MAX, Tim Hortons, and Hilton Hotels and Resorts. There are franchises in all the price ranges, from low cost to millions as an entry fee only.

Purchasing a franchise significantly diminishes the risk of business failure because:

- You are purchasing a tested business model;
- Marketing is sponsored by the franchise owner and covers all the outlets together (as one is selling under the logo/brand of the franchisor);
- You can receive support and training regarding all business aspects (including managerial support);
- You are part of a strong recognized brand, which usually guarantees quality for prospective or actual customers in terms of products and services; and
- You do not need to invest in marketing by yourself.

The downside of it is that most of the famous and world-recognized franchises are costly in terms of entry fee, monthly or

DOI: 10.4324/9781003591429-10

yearly royalty fees, product purchasing, and other requirements. Compliance with the franchisor's strict rules and regulations might hinder growth and does not allow personalization or own marking.

There are franchises in many areas and industries; if you are interested in such a business model, I strongly advise you to study the market well, get a lawyer's advice on compliance documents, and seek expert financial advice on the costs.

Conflicts between the franchisor and franchisee might happen during the collaboration; it is worth considering that each party is also aligned to their respective priorities, goals, or agenda. Therefore, it is advisable to identify common objectives and how both parties can contribute to their achievement. In the end, the franchisor–franchisee relationship is a partnership, and wins should be on both sides.

In any type of business, risk assessment and mitigation are essential to the success and smooth running of the business. In business, there are several categories of risks. The biggest risk is the one that has or can have immediate effects on the organization. Some main categories of risks are:

- *Financial risks* that organization might face in terms of financing, planning, cash flow, or payments.
- *People-related risks* referring to paid or unpaid (internship) staff as well. Here, we can consider high turnover, demotivation, and unprofessional managers.
- *Operational risks* refer to activities and services you conduct, including operational machinery, product malfunctioning, and quality issues.
- *Strategic risks* refer to external situations that might affect the business in any major way. Potential new regulations can be a risk to be handled immediately.

To help in comparing franchises, if you are interested in such business model, I would recommend using Table 9.1.

The most resilient 2025 franchises thrive in sectors where systemic rigor meets creative problem-solving: senior care hybrids blending digital health monitoring with personalized service, tech-driven food concepts optimizing menus via real-time data, and eco-conscious models prototyping community-centric

Table 9.1 Business franchise comparative table

Criteria	First Franchise	Second Franchise	Third Franchise	Fourth Franchise
Exclusivity opportunity (for a region or country)				
Entry fee				
Royalties to be paid monthly/ yearly				
Support offered to franchisee				
Exit costs (if any)				
Financing options				
Sales forecast				

Note: You can add other criteria relevant to your situation. In the author's expert opinion, the criteria mentioned here are essential for consideration when assessing a franchise opportunity.

solutions. Design thinking's five-phase approach – empathize, define, ideate, prototype, test – equips entrepreneurs to dissect challenges with surgical precision, whether refining online education platforms through student journey mapping or overhauling HVAC services via IoT-driven diagnostics. In every case, success hinges on partnerships where franchisors provide the playbook and franchisees inject localized ingenuity. So, wield due diligence as your compass and curiosity as your catalyst and build not just a business but a legacy that marries consistency with reinvention. The future belongs to those who scale with discipline *and* innovate with purpose.

Franchising remains a gateway to entrepreneurial success, blending the agility of ownership with the stability of a proven framework. Yet its true power lies not in mere replication but in symbiotic evolution – where franchisors innovate systems and franchisees inject local ingenuity. As you weigh this path, let due diligence be your compass: dissect financials with forensic precision, negotiate terms with collaborative foresight, and align with brands whose values mirror your ambition. Remember, a franchise isn't just a business – it's a partnership where your growth fuels the collective legacy. Choose wisely, act boldly, and build not just for profit but for enduring impact.

Franchising's strength lies in replicating proven systems, but its future demands innovation that respects both brand integrity and local market nuances. Design thinking – with its emphasis on empathy, prototyping, and user-centric problem-solving – provides a framework to navigate this balance. By applying methodologies like empathy mapping to franchisee–franchisor relationships or rapid prototyping to menu adaptations, businesses can address operational risks while fostering creativity. For instance, franchises adopting design thinking might co-create localized marketing campaigns with franchisees (empathizing with regional preferences) or test AI-driven inventory tools (prototyping operational efficiencies), ensuring scalability without sacrificing adaptability.

Design thinking represents 'human-centered techniques to solve problems in a creative and innovative way – in our designs, in our businesses, in our countries, in our lives.'[1] In simple words, design thinking is the method through which you aim to deeply understand the customers and their in-depth needs, refine the challenges they currently face, and search for innovative solutions for these challenges. In design thinking, one must follow the steps, in order, to get the best possible outcome for their challenge or customers' challenge (or problem).

Research[2] (for business purposes) can be defined as a systematic and well-documented process of gathering relevant data and/or information related to your business specificities; the purpose of such an endeavor is to maximize revenue and make informed decisions. All participants should sign a participation consent form detailing the data collection and usage, as well as their rights (including the right to withdraw from the study at any time).

Step 1: *Empathize with the beneficiaries* (people facing the challenge you aim to investigate). Empathy can be done in two ways: engaging with the beneficiaries at all levels and observing them

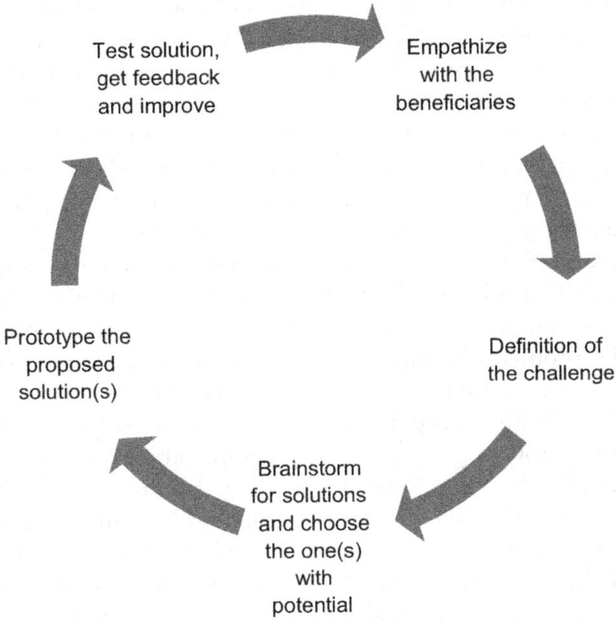

Figure 9.1 Design thinking components.

without engaging with the beneficiaries or people with the problem. The empathy aspect is the foundation of design thinking and must be done properly. In practice, you need to understand the challenge (or the problem) and the people facing it. The engaging aspect can be done through discussions, interviews, or surveys. It is important to take notes and be consistent about it.

Step 2: *Define the challenge* (or problem) as accurately as possible. A clear, concise, and accurate definition will help with other steps, including measuring the result of the process at the end. Let's look at an example:

General definition: *In Barcelona, there are parking issues.* Well, this problem statement is too general, and we can't really focus on the best possible outcome. What kind of parking issues? Where exactly?

Specific definition: *In Barcelona, there is a lack of 100,000 parking spaces in central areas.* In this problem statement, we can note that the issue is very specific, even quantifiable. This will help us with brainstorming for solutions and choosing the most suitable one based on the constraints of the beneficiary.

Step 3: *Brainstorm for solution*(s) and choose the one(s) with potential. The ideal situation is to choose one solution that fits within the constraints and needs of the beneficiaries. By looking at Step 2, we can now brainstorm for focused solutions. We know that we have 100,000 parking places missing; so, what can be done about it? Subterranean parking? Increase the fee for parking so people use more public transportation? Shall we build several floors of parking places to fluid the circulation? Based on the budget and land constraints, solutions can be chosen.

Step 4: *Prototype the proposed solution(s).* We craft a prototype so we can ask for feedback from beneficiaries or users. A prototype can be a sketch, a 3D representation, a simulation, a design, or any graphic representation.

Step 5: *Test the solution, get feedback, and improve the solution.* Once we have the prototype ready, we ask for feedback from the beneficiaries and users. Based on their feedback, we improve our proposed solution, and we ask again for feedback. And the process can go on until the beneficiaries and users are happy with the final version of the solution.

We applied the design thinking process to a product; now it is time to apply it to a service. The situation is more complex because, according to Kotler and Keller (2007), services are intangible, inseparable (from the person delivering it), variable (depending on the person providing it), and perishable (no storage for later usage).

Let's have a look at a practical application of the design thinking process to enhance the student experience at an online university. Online teaching is a service, with the characteristics mentioned before.

Step 1: *Empathize* (interact with students and observations as well). The actions to be done to realize this key step are:

- Conduct virtual focus groups with students from various programs and levels.
- Distribute comprehensive surveys about the online learning experience.

- Analyze student support ticket data and frequently asked questions.
- Shadow online tutors and course facilitators during live sessions.
- Create journey maps of the student experience from enrolment to graduation.
- Collect and analyze dropout rates and reasons for discontinuation.

Step 2: *Define* as accurately as possible the challenge you wish to investigate. The actions to be done to realize this step are:

- Synthesize research findings to identify key pain points (e.g., feelings of isolation, difficulty in time management, technical issues).
- Develop student personas representing different types of online learners (e.g., working professionals, full-time students, international students).
- Craft a problem statement: 'Part-time working students need a flexible and engaging online learning environment that allows them to balance their studies with work and personal commitments while feeling connected to their peers and instructors.'

Step 3: *Ideate* (brainstorm the ideas and then select the most promising one). The actions to be done to realize this step are:

- Organize virtual brainstorming sessions with faculty, instructional designers, and IT staff.
- Use 'what if' scenarios to generate innovative ideas (e.g., 'What if students could customize their entire learning schedule?').
- Explore technological solutions like AI-powered study assistants or virtual reality classrooms.
- Consider community-building initiatives such as virtual study groups or mentorship programs.
- Brainstorm ways to gamify the learning experience to increase engagement.

Step 4: *Prototype* the solution you propose. The actions to be done to realize this key step are:

- Develop a mock-up of a new student dashboard with personalized learning paths.

- Create a prototype of a mobile app for on-the-go learning and community engagement.
- Design a sample curriculum that incorporates more interactive and collaborative elements.
- Draft new guidelines for instructors on facilitating engaging online discussions.
- Sketch out a virtual campus environment using VR technology.

Step 5A: *Test* the proposed solution. The actions to be done to realize this step are:

- Implement the new student dashboard with a small cohort of students.
- Conduct beta testing of the mobile app with a diverse group of learners.
- Pilot the revised curriculum in select courses and gather student feedback.
- Have instructors trial the new discussion facilitation techniques and report on effectiveness.
- Set up a VR demo station for students to experience and provide feedback on the virtual campus concept.

Step 5B: *Implement and iterate.* The actions to be done to realize this step are:

- Analyze test results and refine the chosen solutions.
- Develop a phased implementation plan for the most promising improvements.
- Provide training for faculty and staff on new technologies and teaching methodologies.
- Roll out changes gradually, starting with a pilot program in one department.
- Establish a continuous feedback loop with students, faculty, and staff for ongoing improvements.

By applying this design thinking process, the online university can create a more engaging, flexible, and effective learning environment tailored to the unique needs of its diverse student body. This approach ensures that improvements are grounded in real student experiences and are thoroughly tested before full-scale implementation.

How can one use the design thinking method in practice? Well, it is quite easy: Follow the step-by-step process and do it well. It can be helpful to uncover insights into the needs of potential or existing customers, improve products and services, and improve processes within a company or start-up.

Franchising offers the blueprint, but design thinking ignites the spark of reinvention – a fusion where proven systems meet human-centered innovation. As you step into this dual landscape, remember: success isn't about choosing between structure and creativity but orchestrating their dance. Let franchising's framework ground you and design thinking's empathy propel you. Forge partnerships where franchisors and franchisees co-create, where data sharpens intuition, and where every constraint becomes a catalyst for smarter solutions. The future of business belongs to those who dare to scale with discipline *and* disrupt with purpose. So, wield due diligence as your shield and curiosity as your sword and build not just a franchise but a legacy that thrives on both consistency and reinvention. The path is clear – now march boldly.

NOTES

1 The definition was issued by Interaction Design Foundation and is quoted with their permission. See www.interaction-design.org/

2 To clarify a frequent confusion: searching for information on Google is not the same as doing research.

10

ZERO TO UNICORN

The accelerator playbook for building billion-dollar startups

The growth and sustainable development of start-ups are the healthy backbone of any economic system; they also play a key role in global economic indices. Setting up new businesses contributes to economic development by creating jobs and generating revenue through a variety of taxes. Furthermore, the relevance of start-ups to a country's economy is not vital. Start-up businesses are usually extremely risky, with high growth potential, and government support measures (financial and non-financial) are vital for early-stage companies' survival. SMEs usually face significant challenges due to their lack of experience and know-how, budget constraints, ineffective marketing strategies, lack of networking, and/or poor mentorship. The concept of business incubation links technology, capital, and know-how to harness entrepreneurial flair, accelerate startup development, and, consequently, expedite the commissioned technology.

One obvious important function of start-ups is that they stimulate economic activity in a county, which further leads to the expansion of the country's economy, which also often leads to a higher standard of living for the country's citizens. It has also been observed that start-ups help to boost the technological development of nations. This is so because it encourages innovation among the companies in the locality. The need to compete favorably will lead to innovations among start-ups that will ultimately improve service delivery.

DOI: 10.4324/9781003591429-11

As important and relevant as start-ups are to an economy, it is fairly obvious that quite a few of them do not survive beyond the first few months of their existence. The reason for this is often down to two major factors: leadership gaps and managerial inexperience. As a subset of a lack of proper management, there are other factors such as lack of trust, lack of motivation, lack of requisite knowledge on the method of operating a specific business venture, lack of mentorship, poor product–market fit, uncompetitive pricing, and lack of sound financial management. Also, there are some factors that could potentially lead to the collapse of a business venture regardless of the best efforts of the entrepreneur. Factors such as the lack of demand for the products and services of a company, lack of finance, strong competition, lack of a viable business model, poor pricing, ineffective marketing strategy, and substandard product or service may either stunt the development of a start-up or kill it off altogether.

Start-ups need support in their early stages, and one such support institution is business incubators. The term 'incubator' was derived from the initial meaning of the term, the process of artificially nurturing chicken eggs to hatch them faster in a sheltered environment. A business incubator speeds up early-stage venture creation and significantly increases their success chances. A business incubator boosts new ideas by providing ventures with tangible (physical) and intangible (know-how and services) resources.

Most business incubators are focused primarily on mentoring their growing customer businesses and ensuring their stability both in the short and long run. One of the major features of business incubators is office space. The provision of office space is a fundamental element, and this is because business incubators must necessarily provide a conducive environment, allowing new and already established businesses still trying to find their feet in the industry to accelerate their growth to the point of stability. The plan is that after these businesses have been helped to stand firm, they can then be left alone to fend for themselves. After a start-up has been incubated and is now viable and ready for operation on its own, the link with managed workspaces created earlier is still of relevance. The main aim of a business incubator is the provision of a viable support system for entrepreneurs and their new business ventures through a combination of services that may include mentoring, networking, and shared resources. The purpose of this is to speed up the growth and survival rate of start-ups. This category also includes companies in their nascent years that are not yet strong enough and are still prone to instability.

It is impossible to speak of the success of business incubators without discussing the efforts of governments in helping the incubators to grow. In 1982, Walter Plosila was empowered by the Pennsylvania Legislature to craft and implement the Ben Franklin Partnership Program, one of the United States' first comprehensive technology and manufacturing agendas. The Ben Franklin Program's key component was business incubators; it quickly became a model for other states to support business incubation. In addition to this, the American government, upon noticing the positive impacts of business incubators on businesses, including their positive impact on the nation's economy, went a step further to establish the National Business Incubation Association (NBIA). The organization was established in 1985 with the sole aim of providing training and the necessary support (in terms of tools, know-how, and skills) relevant for assisting start-ups and other fledgling SME firms to attain stability in their business and serving as a repository of information in all things relating to incubator management and other attendant issues.

Right from 1959 when the first business incubator was inaugurated in Batavia, NY, many different practices and processes have been fused into it. Really, business incubation itself has attained many successes over the past several years, with varying levels of success across different countries and continents. However, it is pertinent to state that there is no single incubator practice or policy that is effective across the board (i.e., has a guaranteed success rate regardless of the environment it is practiced within). This is necessary to state because there tend to be high expectations from business owners and other stakeholders, who may be easily swayed by the processes of incubation to expect a 100% success rate. It takes the effectiveness of several processes for business incubation to work effectively. For instance, the work ethics and standards of an organization can impact their corporate sustainability so that an organization with a poor work ethic may be unable to survive regardless of the amount of mentorship and best incubation practices it has been subjected to. Also, the quality of their products or services is also a big factor because quality always attracts patronage. It is rather imperative that prospective business owners be aware of this fact before proceeding to sign up to begin the processes of business incubation.

On one end, it can be argued that there is no ultimate business incubator practice that guarantees absolute success. However, one fact remains, and this is the fact that there are some common practices instituted by most successful organizations, which can serve as a template for start-ups to imbibe and incorporate. Business incubation programs that excel often share similar management and business model practices. As is widely known, the secret of successful entrepreneurs is in their practices. It is helpful that customers can be assessed and reviewed before making any agreement. This will help cut down the number of bad business deals and will help the organization concentrate more on customers who are really in need of their services. Aside from this, there is a need to ensure the incorporation of a flexible payment plan. In the business world, the customer is king. The organization is merely an employee of the customer; after all, without the client, no business can survive. One factor that discourages business patronage is pricing. This is so strong that it determines the level of patronage as well as profitability and sustainability in the long run. Successful businesses have mastered this craft, and most have found a way to charge pocketbook-friendly prices for their products and services and, in some cases, have a flexible payment plan where customers can pay installments. Of course, this approach is not without its risks, but in most cases, it has proven useful and has increased the mass appeal of most organizations. This implies that more customers of varying socio-economic statuses can now subscribe to the products and services of their choice.

Just as incubation in its ordinary form has phases, business incubation is also delineated into several phases. The three phases of business incubation are the foundation, development, and mature incubation phases. These phases are connected to each other, and they develop from one stage to another (i.e., from the foundational phase to the developmental phase and then finally to the mature phase). The three phases are aligned in such a way to help new businesses set up properly and be positioned to properly cater to the needs of their customers:

Foundation Phase – This is the initial stage of business incubation, and it usually commences even before the incubation begins. The core function of business incubators is that small businesses don't die out; hence, there are a range of services provided to ensure that start-ups succeed as much as possible, and the set of actions to ensure this goal begins at the foundation phase.

The foundation phase is essential in making the other two phases work. This is the foundation of the business incubation process, and if the foundational phase is not properly structured, then it could jeopardize the entire process of business incubation. The foundation phase includes planning and feasibility studies. It also includes raising funds, marketing the company's products and services, building relationships within the organizations, assembling the right team to achieve its purpose, determining the legal type of company, and so on. Basically, anyone with an idea can be part of the foundation stage. Such an individual can be invited to share their ideas with the incubators. In the foundation phase, activities are coordinated, and decisions made will positively affect the immediate environment in that they will solve a need.

In short, the foundation stage of business incubation is the stage where ideas are screened and refined. Guided mentoring is thereafter embarked upon to further prune the idea and make it practicable and actionable. Other features of the foundation stage include technical assistance to further develop the prototype, after which there is a progressive evaluation as regard moving on to the next phase. In the foundation phase, there is also the need to ensure that there is functional access to the internet, as this will simplify the process and make it more efficient when recourse can be made to the internet to source more ideas and concepts to ensure the success of the business incubation. All the activities in the foundation phase are coordinated to ensure there is capacity building and proper networking to facilitate the growth of the business.

Development Phase – The developmental stage kicks in automatically upon the completion of the foundation stage. This phase is more complex than the previous stage, and it involves actionable steps on some of the ideas conceived at the foundation stage. In short, this is the stage where actions are tested and implemented. It is at this phase that the prototype developed at the previous stage will be tested. At the start, the incubators will focus on developing and implementing effective marketing strategies, building partnerships, creating a strong network, and reaching a critical mass of participating companies to secure a positive cash flow. Once these activities are completed, incubators begin to operate, seeking to influence the outcomes and growth of the wider economic area. A workable and practical revenue model is developed for the business at this stage, and a range of support services is developed for the business to prime it for full-scale operations. Post-graduation, incubators follow up with their former participating companies for up to five years; the incubator also involves them in the future program, mentoring new firms and aiding in know-how creation. This can also be the time when many of the tax incentives, subsidies, and other benefits that the business participating company's managerial team relied upon will expire or decrease, requiring the incubatee to ensure other forms of funding and/or revenue streams available. At the completion of majority of the developmental stage, it is expected that the business will have begun to receive orders for their products or services. This is because, for the business to move to the maturation stage, it must necessarily have started receiving orders and consequently be slowly building its customer base.

Mature Incubation Phase – This is the final stage of the incubation cycle. At this stage, it is expected that the participating companies have received a lot of services geared toward improving their chances of survival, as well as sustainability in the long run. At this stage, it is required that business incubators demonstrate their socio-economic impact on the community and/or wider economy through the successful graduation of participating companies. The participating companies at this stage are strong and nourished enough to stay healthy and stand strong. Mature incubators most often will go further by exploring the prospect of offering support services, learning, and training opportunities for participating companies. Although this is the graduation stage where participating companies are meant to be left alone, most incubators often attempt to connect their participating companies with their alumni network to ensure a connection is maintained even after the official completion of the incubation process. This, therefore, implies that the incubation process can be an ongoing process that will last for a considerable time such that it can continue to expand further, even as new participating companies are taken in and mentored and then released into the network to maintain continuity and sustainability. On a final note, it is expected that at the maturation stage, each participating company will have access to an official space from which their business will be formally operating. They are also expected to have received strategic support as well as financing platforms where they can access funds to ensure the smooth running of their businesses. The hallmark of incubation is mentoring and coaching; hence, each participating company must have been mentored by an experienced professional operating within the same industry or at least a similar industry. For instance, Dropbox credits Y Combinator's mentorship for refining its freemium model, which grew its user base from 100,000 to 4 million during incubation. It is a major requirement of the 21st-century business environment that businesses have access to legal, financial, and advisory support systems, as these will certainly be needed at some point in the business operations. This is why, prior to the completion of the incubation agreement, all of these support strategies must have been made ready for the business to operate without a hitch and sustain itself for the years to come. It must be noted that even after undergoing the process of incubation, it may not necessarily mean that the business venture is certain to survive. There are still chances that it might not survive, but what is also certain is that business incubation contributes significantly to the survival rates of new businesses worldwide.

Business accelerators are another extremely useful tool to boost firms' growth with a minimum viable product, while an incubator is focused on flushing out business ideas with the potential of success. The incubation period for a business accelerator is usually 6 months. The accelerators provide extensive know-how in several areas such as training, financing, prototyping, and market studies.

Business accelerators have emerged as vital components of the global startup ecosystem, offering structured programs designed to rapidly propel early-stage companies towards success. These programs typically last 3–6 months, providing a combination of seed investment, mentorship, educational components, and networking opportunities.

Criteria	Incubators	Accelerators
Focus	Early-stage idea validation	Scaling proven MVPs
Duration	1–5 years	3–6 months
Funding	Rarely equity based	Seed investment for equity (5–10%)
Outcome	Business stability	Rapid growth and investor connections

Key characteristics of business accelerators

1. Cohort based: Startups are admitted in batches, fostering peer learning and community.
2. Fixed-term: Programs have a defined start and end date, creating urgency and focus.
3. Mentorship driven: Experienced entrepreneurs and industry experts provide guidance.
4. Culminates in a 'demo day': Startups pitch to investors at the program's conclusion.
5. Seed investment: Often provide initial funding in exchange for equity, typically 5–10%.

Global examples of successful accelerators

1. Y Combinator (USA):
   - Notable recent outcomes: Stripe, Brex, Deel (all valued over $1 billion)
   - Investment: $500,000 ($125,000 for 7% equity, $375,000 on uncapped safe)
   - Acceptance rate: <1.5%
2. Startupbootcamp (Europe):
   - Locations: Multiple cities across Europe
   - Recent success: Tink (acquired by Visa for $2.1 billion in 2021)
   - Investment: €15,000 for 6–8% equity
   - Programs: FinTech, InsurTech, Smart City, and IoT

3. Startup Chile (South America):
   - Location: Santiago, Chile
   - Notable alumni: Cornershop (acquired by Uber for $459 million in 2021)
   - Investment: Up to $80,000 equity-free
   - Focus: Attracting global startups to Chile
4. JFDI.Asia (Asia):
   - Location: Singapore
   - Notable success: Tradegecko (acquired by Intuit for $80 million in 2020).
   - Investment: S$50,000 for 8.88% equity
   - Focus: Deep tech startups in Southeast Asia
5. iHub (Africa):
   - Location: Nairobi, Kenya
   - Notable startups: Ushahidi, BRCK
   - Investment: Varies by program
   - Focus: Technology innovation in Africa
6. Antler (Global):
   - Locations: Multiple cities worldwide
   - Recent success: Xanpool (raised $41 million in 2022)
   - Investment: $110,000 for 10% equity
   - Focus: Building startups from scratch with talented individuals

As with any investment, accelerators have established some key performance indicators (KPIs):

1. Portfolio company valuation growth.
2. Funding raised by portfolio companies post-program.
3. Revenue growth of portfolio companies.
4. Job creation by portfolio companies.
5. Survival rate of portfolio companies.
6. Successful exits (acquisitions or IPOs).

Accelerators play a crucial role in the global startup ecosystem by providing resources, connections, and expertise that significantly increase a startup's chances of success. They bridge the gap between early-stage ideas and venture capital funding, helping startups refine their business models, build strong teams, and achieve product-market fit. The latest trends are digital accelerators, where everything is happening online. Techstars Anywhere (2017) and 500 Startups' virtual programs (2020) now serve founders in 150+ countries, democratizing access to accelerator resources.

The global nature of accelerators has led to the cross-pollination of ideas and the creation of truly international startups. For example, Startup Chile has attracted entrepreneurs from over 80 countries, fostering a diverse and innovative startup community in Latin America. Similarly, Antler's global presence allows it to tap into talent pools worldwide, creating startups with international perspectives from day one.

As the startup ecosystem continues to evolve, accelerators are adapting to meet new challenges. Many are now offering virtual programs, expanding their reach beyond geographical boundaries. Others are specializing in specific industries or technologies, providing more targeted support to startups in areas like AI, blockchain, or clean energy.

The impact of accelerators extends beyond individual startups. They play a significant role in developing entrepreneurial ecosystems in their respective regions, attracting talent and capital, and fostering innovation. As such, they have become important drivers of economic growth and technological advancement worldwide.

Business incubators and accelerators stand as launchpads for entrepreneurial ambition – transforming raw ideas into resilient enterprises through structured mentorship, resource access, and global networks. While no program guarantees immunity from failure, these ecosystems dramatically tilt the odds in favor of founders bold enough to iterate, adapt, and persist. As you embark on your venture, remember: The most groundbreaking innovations often emerge from the intersection of audacious vision and collaborative support. Whether through physical hubs or digital cohorts, today's tools empower you to build not just a business but a legacy that reshapes industries and elevates communities. The journey demands grit, but with the right systems amplifying your efforts, even moonshot ideas gain gravitational pull. Now is the time to lean into these accelerants – your blueprint for growth awaits.

11

THE ALGORITHMIC ADVANTAGE

Cutting costs, boosting speed, winning markets

In today's rapidly evolving business landscape, organizations are increasingly turning to advanced technologies to enhance efficiency, streamline processes, and gain a competitive edge. This chapter explores how businesses can leverage artificial intelligence (AI), digitalization, automation, and blockchain technology to optimize their operations and drive growth.

Artificial intelligence has emerged as a powerful tool for businesses to enhance their operational efficiency and decision-making processes. By leveraging AI technologies, companies can automate routine tasks, gain valuable insights from data, and improve customer experiences.

Automating Routine Tasks: Artificial intelligence serves as a transformative force in operational streamlining, systematically converting manual workflows into efficient digital processes. By assuming responsibility for high-volume, low-complexity activities – such as database management and initial client communications – AI reallocates human capital toward cognitively demanding initiatives requiring strategic thinking. Modern conversational interfaces exemplify this shift, where intelligent virtual assistants resolve 73% of routine service requests in under 12 seconds, enabling customer care teams to concentrate on nuanced technical support and relationship-building scenarios. This operational redistribution creates a dual productivity impact: enhancing procedural throughput while elevating workforce value generation.

DOI: 10.4324/9781003591429-12

Advanced Data Analytics: AI empowers businesses to extract valuable insights from large datasets efficiently. AI-driven data analytics can personalize offerings and predict future trends by analyzing customer behavior across various touchpoints. This enhances marketing strategies and customer engagement by increasing business efficiency. Furthermore, AI can scour online sources like social media and news articles to identify emerging market trends, enabling businesses to stay agile and proactive in decision-making.

Personalized Customer Experiences: AI enables businesses to deliver highly personalized customer experiences by analyzing vast amounts of customer data. For instance, AI algorithms can analyze purchase history, browsing behavior, and demographic information to provide tailored product recommendations, personalized marketing messages, and customized user interfaces. This level of personalization can significantly enhance customer satisfaction and loyalty.

Employee Productivity Enhancement: AI enhances employee productivity by automating mundane tasks and providing intelligent support tools. For example, AI-powered virtual assistants can schedule meetings, prioritize emails, and generate reports, freeing up time for employees to focus on higher-value tasks requiring human creativity and problem-solving skills. AI can also facilitate personalized learning and development programs by recommending training modules based on individual employee performance and career goals.

AI technology can be used based on prompts. These prompts should have three fundamental characteristics: provide context that is as detailed as possible, wishes and constraints, the required format and the desired tone. In Appendix 2, you can find several prompts useful for an entrepreneur.

Next, it is time to talk about two concepts that you might have heard often: digitization and digitalization (often used interchangeably).

Digitization refers to the process of converting analog information into a digital format. It's essentially about transforming physical data (like text, images, and sounds) into digital bits and bytes that can be processed by computers. Examples of digitization include:

- Converting physical documents or photographs into digital files (like PDFs or JPEGs) through scanning.
- Transforming analog audio and video recordings (like cassette tapes and VHS) into digital formats (like MP3 and MP4).
- Transcribing information from paper forms into computer-readable formats.

Digitalization involves leveraging digital technologies to transform business processes, create new business models, and enhance customer experiences. It's about using digitized data and digital tools to simplify and improve operations. Examples of digitalization include:

- Implementing e-procurement software to streamline purchasing processes and improve spend visibility.
- Adopting cloud-based solutions to reduce IT infrastructure costs and enhance collaboration.
- Utilizing data analytics for better decision-making and cost control.

To contrast these two terms often used with the same meaning, I would like to point out that digitization focuses on data conversion, and digitalization represents a paradigm shift in business operations: for instance, a hospital digitizing patient records (digitization) versus using AI-powered analytics to predict treatment outcomes (digitalization).

BUSINESS PROCESS AUTOMATION: STRATEGIES FOR STARTUPS

Business process automation (BPA) is particularly crucial for startups, as it allows them to scale operations efficiently and compete with larger, more established companies. Here are key strategies for implementing BPA in startups:

1. *Define Clear Business Goals:* Before implementing automation, startups should clearly define their business goals and identify which processes, if automated, would contribute

most significantly to achieving these goals. This might include increasing efficiency, reducing costs, improving customer satisfaction, or scaling operations.

2. *Start With Core Processes:* Begin by pinpointing operational bottlenecks characterized by high-frequency repetition, manual intensity, and error susceptibility. Key candidates typically involve:

    - Client Onboarding Sequences: Identity verification and service activation workflows.
    - Financial Reconciliation Systems: Vendor payment processing and expense auditing.
    - Asset Tracking Mechanisms: Real-time stock level monitoring across multiple channels.
    - Workforce Integration Protocols: New hire documentation and system access provisioning.

3. *Choose Suitable Tools for Your Business:* Select those tools that align with your specific needs and integrate well with your existing systems. Consider factors such as scalability, ease of use, and cost-effectiveness. Popular automation tools for startups include Zapier for workflow automation, HubSpot for marketing automation, Asana for workflow automation (e.g., automating task assignments based on project stage), or Jira for software development teams to auto-generate tickets from bug reports.
4. *Implement Gradually:* Start with a pilot project to test the automation solution and gather feedback. This approach allows for adjustments and helps ensure a smooth transition. Gradually expand automation to other processes as you gain experience and confidence.
5. *Train and Engage Employees:* Ensure that employees are properly trained on new automated systems and understand the benefits of automation. Engage them in the process to gain buy-in and valuable insights for improvement.
6. *Monitor and Optimize:* Regularly review the performance of automated processes and gather feedback from users. Use this information to continually refine and optimize your automation strategies.

STARTUP AUTOMATION ROADMAP

Stage	Action	Tool Example	Impact
1	Core process identification	Process mining software	35% efficiency gain
2	Tool selection matrix	Zapier-QuickBooks integration	50% faster reconciliations
3	Gradual deployment	Asana automation templates	4-week implementation cycle
4	Workforce upskilling	AI-powered LMS platforms	73% adoption rates
5	Performance monitoring	Process analytics dashboards	Real-time KPI tracking
6	Continuous optimization	Machine learning refinements	15% quarterly improvements

DIGITAL PAYMENTS AND BLOCKCHAIN TECHNOLOGY IN BUSINESS

The financial technology sector has seen significant advancements with the rise of digital payments and blockchain technology. These innovations are reshaping how businesses handle transactions and manage financial operations.

Digital payment systems have revolutionized the way businesses process transactions, offering increased speed, security, and convenience. Some key advantages of digital payments include:

- Reduced transaction costs.
- Faster processing times.
- Enhanced security through encryption and tokenization.
- Improved cash flow management.
- Greater accessibility for customers.

Examples of digital payment solutions include:

1. Mobile payment platforms like Apple Pay and Google Pay.
2. Peer-to-peer payment services such as Venmo and PayPal.
3. Contactless payment systems using NFC technology.

However, businesses must address challenges like cybersecurity risks (e.g., phishing attacks targeting digital wallets) and the digital divide limiting access for unbanked populations.

Blockchain technology offers a decentralized and secure way to record and verify transactions. Its applications in business extend beyond cryptocurrencies, providing opportunities for enhanced transparency, security, and efficiency in various processes. Key applications of blockchain in business include:

1. *Supply Chain Management:* Blockchain can provide end-to-end visibility and traceability in supply chains. For example, Walmart uses blockchain technology to track its supply chain, ensuring food safety and streamlining supplier payments.
2. *Smart Contracts*: These self-executing contracts with the terms of the agreement directly written into code can automate and enforce contract terms, reducing the need for intermediaries and minimizing disputes.
3. *Cross-Border Payments*: Blockchain enables faster and more cost-effective international transactions. For instance, companies like Santander use RippleNet for cross-border payments, reducing settlement times from days to minutes. However, adoption challenges persist, including regulatory uncertainty and interoperability issues between legacy banking systems.
4. *Identity Verification:* Blockchain can provide secure and efficient identity verification solutions, reducing fraud and streamlining know-your-customer (KYC) processes.
5. *Loyalty Programs:* Blockchain-based loyalty programs can offer more transparency and flexibility. Singapore Airlines' KrisFlyer loyalty program uses blockchain technology to provide a digital wallet for members to manage and spend their miles more efficiently.

To illustrate the practical applications of these technologies, let's examine some real-world examples of companies successfully leveraging AI and automation:

1. *Amazon – AI-Driven Inventory Management and Logistics:* Amazon uses AI algorithms to predict customer demand, optimize

inventory levels, and streamline its logistics operations. This has resulted in significant cost savings and improved delivery times for the e-commerce giant.

2. *Netflix – Personalized Content Recommendations:* Netflix's AI-powered recommendation system analyzes user viewing habits to provide personalized content suggestions. This has led to increased user engagement and reduced churn rates.
3. *Starbucks – AI-Enhanced Customer Experience:* Starbucks uses AI to personalize its mobile app experience, offering tailored product recommendations and promotions based on individual customer preferences and purchase history.
4. *UiPath – Robotic Process Automation for Business Efficiency*: UiPath, a leading provider of robotic process automation (RPA) solutions, has helped numerous companies automate repetitive tasks. For instance, UiPath helped Verizon automate 85% of its customer onboarding tasks, reducing manual errors by 60% and saving 10,000+ annual work hours.

The integration of AI, digitalization, automation, and blockchain technology offers businesses unprecedented opportunities to optimize operations, enhance customer experiences, and drive growth. By strategically implementing these technologies, companies can streamline processes, make data-driven decisions, and gain a competitive edge in today's digital landscape.

However, it's crucial to approach these technological advancements with a clear strategy aligned with business goals. Organizations should carefully assess their needs, start with pilot projects, and continuously refine their approaches based on feedback and results.

As these technologies continue to evolve, businesses that successfully leverage them will be well positioned to thrive in an increasingly digital and competitive marketplace. In navigating this technological frontier, businesses must balance innovation with intentionality:

- *AI*: Prioritize ethical data use over surveillance.
- *Automation*: Augment human labor, don't replace it.
- *Blockchain*: Focus on solving tangible pain points, not tech for tech's sake.

By anchoring decisions in customer needs and employee wellbeing, organizations can harness technology as a force for sustainable growth.

We cannot conclude this section without discussing hybrid business models. Contemporary organizations are progressively implementing hybrid operational frameworks that synergize physical infrastructure with digital capabilities. These models enable enterprises to maximize asset utilization while addressing varied consumer preferences through technological integration. Major retailers exemplify this approach, such as Target's fusion of AI-driven stock management systems with curbside collection services, demonstrating how digital precision enhances physical convenience. Starbucks exemplifies the hybrid model by merging its physical cafés with advanced digital infrastructure. Its 'Digital Flywheel' strategy integrates mobile ordering, AI-driven inventory systems, and blockchain-enabled loyalty rewards, allowing customers to pre-order via app and collect via curbside pickup while maintaining in-store experiences like barista interactions. Both companies demonstrate how hybrid models balance efficiency with human-centric experiences, using tools like cloud analytics and smart contracts to unify operational channels without sacrificing brand identity.

Strategic benefits of hybrid systems in business:

Adaptive Resource Management: Enterprises gain capacity to shift assets between operational channels dynamically. Financial institutions have achieved 40% reduction in physical office footprints while sustaining service standards through AI-assisted customer support platforms and virtual consultancy teams.

Expanded Market Penetration: Dual-channel strategies accommodate both digitally native and traditional consumer segments. Walmart's mobile scanning application permits in-store patrons to circumvent conventional checkout queues, complementing their digital fulfillment infrastructure that processes online orders.

Cost-Efficiency Balance: Emerging businesses implement automation solutions like workflow integrators for backend operations while preserving artisanal customer interactions. This equilibrium minimizes operational expenditures without compromising unique value propositions.

Effective hybrid models require interconnected digital ecosystems:

Unified Communication Platforms: Enterprise collaboration tools facilitate synchronous coordination between distributed teams and headquarters staff through integrated chat, document sharing, and video conferencing capabilities.

Predictive Resource Allocation: Machine learning systems process multichannel operational data to optimize stock distribution, exemplified by food service chains forecasting demand differentials between walk-in customers and delivery orders.

Decentralized Logistics Networks: Blockchain-enabled supply chains employ self-executing contracts to harmonize inventory tracking systems with distribution applications, enhancing transparency across hybrid operational nodes.

Structured hybrid frameworks prove particularly effective in workforce management, with technology firms implementing fixed office schedules complemented by remote work flexibility. This approach sustains organizational culture while accessing broader talent pools, reflected in 30% improved staff retention metrics compared to fully virtual operations

As we stand at the intersection of human ingenuity and technological advancement, businesses face not just a choice but an imperative: to harness AI, automation, and blockchain not as isolated tools but as interconnected forces reshaping commerce. The organizations that will dominate tomorrow's markets are those that view technology as a *strategic compass* rather than a quick fix – embedding ethical AI into decision-making frameworks, designing hybrid operations that amplify human potential, and building blockchain infrastructures that prioritize transparency over hype. Success will belong to leaders who wield these technologies with surgical precision: automating not merely to cut costs but to unlock creativity; analyzing data not to chase trends but to anticipate unmet human needs; digitizing not for novelty but to forge unbreakable trust with stakeholders. The future favors those who recognize that in our algorithm-driven age, sustainable competitive advantage springs from marrying machine efficiency with distinctly human virtues – empathy, intuition, and the courage to innovate responsibly.

12

THE RESILIENT ENTREPRENEUR

Launching with contracts, clauses, and contingency plans

This is the final lap in the race to start your business. Choosing a representative name could also be a challenge. I am convinced each one of us would like to see their names on a business, but this is not the best choice in most cases (except if the name is well known and recognized). The name of the company should be related in some way to the activities you plan to do with your company.

Before starting, you need to decide on the type of business (legal form) you wish to start. You should assess the pros and cons for each category and consider the process and costs of setting and closing it (suitable for the planning phase and in case of need).

For start-ups, the most suitable forms of businesses are:

1. *Sole Proprietorship* – a type of business run by someone for their own benefit. It is the simplest way of doing business (some countries might regulate which categories of business you can set up in through such a legal form), with low registration costs, quick registration, money available at one's own disposal anytime, and a simple accountancy system (one can even do it by oneself). The biggest downside of this type of business is that the owner is 100% liable (with all personal assets) for all the debts of the company.
2. *LLC or Limited Liability Company* – the main advantage is that the owner's liability is limited to the company's assets and resources. You can do almost any type of business through such

DOI: 10.4324/9781003591429-13

a legal entity; you will need an accountant to do your bookkeeping. Taxes will be different for such entities depending on the country in which you will be located, specific domain of activity, mainland, or free zone residence.

Countries like the UAE (via its 'Virtual Company License') and Estonia ('e-Residency' program) offer e-licenses, enabling remote business operations with tax advantages. Compare these options based on your target market and residency needs. In such situations, taxation is also advantageous, so it is recommended to compare opportunities based on your priorities. This type of business is a fast, low-cost setting and might allow you to reside in a specific country for a limited amount of time. It is worth considering based on your priorities and specific situation.

When you are convinced that you already have the resources to start the business, don't just go ahead and start it immediately. It is time to do the next steps:

1. *Register your business*
   This is a very important step if you want your business to be recognized. You must register it with the government so that it will become officially recognized as a business entity. Each country has different procedures, so you should check with your local Chamber of Commerce or similar entity for business registration. In many countries, these entities offer free or low-cost consultancy for the registration process. Some countries offer two different company registrations – one the mainland and the other in the so-called 'free economic zones.' Depending on your interest and serving market, you should weigh the options well.
2. *Get an insurance policy*[1]
   Don't forget to do this before you launch your business. You may have to contend with theft, property damage, or lawsuits from customers in the future. These unethical and illegal practices may be very expensive and may negatively affect your business. An insurance policy will cushion the effect of such lawsuits and other damages/losses on your business.

   If you will hire employees, you may have to purchase unemployment policy and workers' compensation as the minimum insurance policy. If you want to block potential loopholes, you can purchase general liability insurance. A business owner's policy is another option for you. You should consult different insurance agents or brokers to identify the suitable policy for your situation.

3. *Create your brand and market it*

   There is no sense in starting a business without creating prior awareness about the business. It is this awareness that will serve as an appetizer to potential customers. There are two ways of doing this: create a website for your brand and leverage social media.

   If you want to create a website for your brand, bear in mind the need for you to have a logo for your brand. Use this logo across all the social media sites where you have a presence for your brand. People will be conscious of this logo and identify it with your brand. Whenever you are ready to launch your brand, give incentives to potential customers by giving them coupons that they can use to make online purchases. Coupons should align with customer acquisition goals. For example, a '20% off first order' email campaign can convert social media followers into buyers, while loyalty points encourage repeat purchases.

The fact that you have launched your business doesn't mean that you can now sit down and relax, hoping for miracles to happen. Instead of doing that, do whatever is possible to grow the business to keep the business going and profitable.

If you want to do this, you can network with others in the same business niche as you. Make use of established bloggers to give you the right promotion with the promise of giving them some products or services in exchange for that. If there are charity organizations that you know, partner with them and support them in your own way. If you can do these things, your brand will continue to be recognized and will grow with time.

While branding builds visibility, formal partnerships require legal safeguards. Well-structured contracts protect your business as you scale. In the most common situations, any partnership is established based on a contract with clear contractual terms, rights and obligations, duration, and additional clauses. It is highly recommended to seek the assistance of a lawyer once such a contract needs to be set in place. In the following, I discuss the most common contractual terms that any entrepreneur should know.

The mutual protection afforded by a well-drafted contract between a firm and its customer cannot be overstated. They create a lawful instrument that secures the fundamentals, such as payments, and they define clear objectives for both sides so that there is no misunderstanding. Nevertheless, contracts are useless if they lack the necessary provisions to provide transparency to both parties and security to you. Many people fail to do this, instead contentedly using a one-size-fits-all template they discovered online.

A *contract* must clarify the parties involved in it on both sides, along with witnesses. While the specifics of any contract will change based on the nature of the business, the interests of the parties involved, and the tasks at hand, several provisions should be present in every agreement you submit or execute.

Your competence to guarantee that your contracts effectively reflect your financial dealings, fully protect your interests, and minimize your liabilities is a critical factor in determining the success of your company, regardless of the size of your company.

Transparently defined rights and obligations – Your company contracts should outline the rights and responsibilities of each person involved in the transaction or agreement. Your contract should provide a detailed explanation of the conditions that have been agreed upon so that all parties are aware of their obligations. For example, if a company is purchasing goods from a supplier, all rights to receive the product and obligation to pay a certain amount of money should be clear in the contract.

Payment stipulations – Contracts that are worth their salt will include all the pertinent details regarding monetary obligations. You should specify when, exactly, throughout the project's duration you will deliver the bill and when, exactly, after that, you will anticipate payment. For example, if a project is 1 year long, the number of installments and due date for each installment must be mentioned.

Safeguards against disclosure – It is possible to include as many specifics as you like in a secrecy provision. The most basic one will promise not to disclose any details about the customer to any third party. In extreme situations, you may be prohibited from disclosing even the fact that you formerly worked for the business, let alone any confidential information about its finances, activities, or the like.

Liability allocation – Every business owner needs to give serious thought to the issues of liability. Clearly define which party bears responsibility for legal disputes arising from the work. For example, a software developer might limit liability to the cost of services rendered, excluding indirect damages.

If at all possible, it is recommended that both your company and the customer have some form of commercial or legal insurance to safeguard yourselves and your associates. The real world isn't perfect, and some customers may try to pass the buck or put the responsibility on you. Plan so you know what is expected of you, the extent of your potential liability, and the measures you may take to mitigate it.

Clauses of termination – Many company leaders overlook this crucial provision and later regret that they did not include it in their contracts.

An assignment agreement – For instance, a termination clause in a freelance contract might allow either party to exit with 30 days' notice, prorating payments for work completed.

Dispute clauses, which outline how disagreements on the project will be settled, can be included in a contract just as termination clauses. You may find this in conjunction with a termination provision in some contracts; the idea is to provide an opportunity to work out any problems before the contract can be officially terminated.

Before signing any contract, either one that was drafted by your attorney or sent to you by a customer, you should ensure that it does not adversely affect you or place you in jeopardy. Take the time to read it over and make sure you grasp its meaning. If you are the founder of a service firm, you should resist accepting any contracts that have non-compete restrictions that could hurt your chances of acquiring new customers in the future. While some may make sense, the vast majority will severely limit your company's expansion possibilities, particularly if you're operating in a narrow market.

In this section, I share some general business advice based on the extensive experience I have with businesses. Please note that this advice must be considered in the context of your particular situation and not just as a separate matter. Whenever you need support, do not hesitate to ask for it. External perspectives and another set of eyes might bring new perspectives and ideas.

1. Split the shares of the company in such a way that one person (or a group of interests) has *the majority of shares (majority of shares means owning at least 50.1% of the shares)*. The reason behind this is that in certain moments, partners will have different views (disagree), and the decision process could be blocked if the shares are split equally. Plenty of businesses have closed because of such disagreements, and they could not move forward; in the beginning, things seem okay, and partners agree on how things will move on, but several factors can affect this irreversibly. In a company, the owner of the majority of shares has the decisive vote (the definitive say) regarding decisions to be made.
2. *Golden rule: Never, ever do business with friends and family*. You can ask for help from time to time if needed, but do not get them legally or formally involved in the decision process. In case you do business with family or friends, separate what happens in the firm from the personal relation by setting a set of clear rules.
3. *Preventive management and financing are another vital key for success.* It is necessary to have a budget to cover the business expenses for at least its first 6 months of existence. Once you have profit, you should save 10% into a separate account for unforeseen events (preventive financial management). In terms of general management, preventive management means thinking ahead about what could go wrong and having backup plans for it. Plan ahead for maintenance, proper insurance, and necessary resources. Always have several suppliers for your vital raw materials or products. Diversify suppliers to avoid disruptions – for example, a bakery might source flour from both local and international vendors to hedge against shortages.
4. In the sales process, getting a NO is not the end of the world; *the NO of today might not still be a NO after few months.* The most

important point to remember is to connect with the person, keep in touch, and, after a while, approach again, focusing on their needs. Do not be aggressive, but be friendly and empathetic and address customers' pains.

5. *Handling work–life balance is essential for your wellbeing.* Establish clear working hours (e.g., 9 AM–6 PM) and disconnect afterward. Early-stage businesses may require longer hours initially, but schedule regular reviews to adjust boundaries. Communicate expectations with clients (e.g., 'Urgent requests after 7 PM incur a 25% surcharge').
6. *Plan and create a community around your business.* This is a long-term goal, and you need to constantly work on this aspect. Online communities are very practical, but some customers prefer in-person connections. It takes time to experiment and find what works for you and your community.
7. *Space entrepreneurship*[2] *(or space economy) is the new frontier or the future normal.* Developed countries are heavily financing enterprises in this regard. For example, the EU, through its European Space Agency (ESA), has a network of space business incubators across Europe; these incubators focus on supporting businesses with space-related businesses and assist them in finding financing.
8. *FabLabs*[3] *or fabrication laboratories are a tool that any entrepreneur should be familiar with.* There is a global net of such labs freely available for assisting entrepreneurs.
9. If any of your commercial contracts involve external shipping of sales or goods, you should specify the transportation and customs fees according to *Incoterms (International Commercial Terms) regulations.* Please note that there are several versions of Incoterms,[4] and you need to specify which year's definition of clauses applies. Incoterms are standardized rules developed by the International Chamber of Commerce (ICC) to define responsibilities between buyers and sellers in international trade. They clarify:

    - *Cost allocation* (who pays for shipping, insurance, customs)
    - *Risk transfer points* (when liability shifts from seller to buyer)
    - *Documentation requirements*

    Over 90% of global trade uses Incoterms to avoid disputes.

10. Entrepreneurs often face a dilemma about the right moment to expand/grow the business. Well, in order to even start assessing the whole situation (the entrepreneur, the business, and the economic context), you must have a valid (and tested) business model, financial resources to cover all the expansion expenses for at least 6 months (12 months would be ideal), and a realistic plan.
11. Leverage technology to *automate* tasks like invoicing (e.g., QuickBooks) or customer outreach (e.g., Mailchimp workflows).
12. A growth mindset is essential for entrepreneurs, as it fuels resilience, innovation, and continuous improvement in the face of challenges. Entrepreneurs with a growth mindset view obstacles as opportunities to learn and grow, enabling them to adapt quickly to market changes, embrace feedback, and persistently pursue their goals despite setbacks. For example, a growth mindset helps pivot a failed product launch into market research for a better-fit offering.
13. There is no perfect plan or document, so do not aim for perfection in this matter; you need to aim for the document suitable for the current situation and update it as needed.

Launching a business is both a milestone and a beginning – a testament to your planning and a call to embrace adaptability. As you move forward, let resilience guide your decisions: refine contracts to protect your vision, leverage LLC safeguards to mitigate risk, and nurture communities that amplify your brand's impact. Remember, entrepreneurship thrives not in perfection but in iterative growth. For ongoing support, resources like FabLabs and ESA incubators offer tangible pathways to scale, while Incoterms clarity ensures global partnerships flourish. Your journey now shifts from preparation to action – equipped with frameworks for legal compliance, preventive management, and mindful leadership.

The road ahead will challenge and reward in equal measure. Stay curious, remain agile, and remember: every 'no' today refines the 'yes' of tomorrow.

NOTES

1 You can get insurance policies anytime during the life of the company. These costs are deductible in your financial statements.
2 More details can be found at https://business.esa.int/
3 More details can be found at www.fablabs.io/
4 More details about Incoterms can be found at https://iccwbo.org/business-solutions/incoterms-rules/incoterms-2020/

APPENDIX 1

Customer persona or avatar[1]

Name:[2]
Bio of your persona: (describe who s/he is, the relationship with the product, pain points, relevant matters for your persona/avatar, etc.)

Demographics

Age	
Gender	
Education level (area of specialization)	
Occupation	
Residence	
Income	
Marital status	

Personal data

Objectives	
Areas of interest(s)	
Pain points (searching to heal a 'pain' or pleasure deriving from the usage of a product/service)	
Information sources	

Experience with the product/service

Level of experience with the product/service	
The need the product/service satisfies	
Frustration with similar products/services	
Wishlist	

Customer persona for a dental clinic – example

Name: Sarah
Bio: Sarah is a 35-year-old working mother of two young children, living in a suburban area. She is health conscious and values her family's wellbeing but struggles to find time for regular dental check-ups due to her busy schedule. Sarah has had negative experiences with dentists in the past, which has led to some anxiety about dental visits. She seeks a family-friendly dental office that would fit her hectic schedule and provide comfort, ensuring no stress for either her or her children.

Demographics

Age	35 years old
Gender	Female
Education level (area of specialization)	Bachelor's degree in marketing
Occupation	Sales manager
Residence	Suburban area
Income	90,000 euros/yearly
Marital status	Married; two children aged 5 and 8

Personal data

Objectives	To maintain good oral health for herself and her family, to overcome dental anxiety, to find a reliable dentist
Areas of interest(s)	Fitness, healthy cooking, family activities, reading

Values	Family, health, work–life balance, efficiency
Challenges	Time management, dental anxiety, balancing work and family responsibilities
Pain points (searching to heal a 'pain' or pleasure deriving from the usage of a product/service)	'Heal a pain' • Can't find appointment times that suit her schedule • Apprehension with dental procedures and the possibility of pain • Worried about making dental visits a positive experience for her children • Cannot visit several times, and she needs to have a one-stop service clinic
Information sources	Formal, official dental clinic website; medical manufacturers; specialized peer-reviewed publications
Preferred communication channel(s)	Emails, WhatsApp messages

Experience with the product/service

Level of experience with the product/service	• Irregular dental check-ups due to busy schedule • Dental anxiety due to past experiences • Concerned about oral health and good habits in children
The need the product/service satisfies	• Flexibility in appointment scheduling, evening and weekend appointments included • Clarity on procedures and associated costs • Child-friendly environment and staff • Gentle and patient-focused approach to alleviate anxiety • Modern technology for efficient and comfortable treatments

Frustration with similar products/services	• Can't find appointment times that suit her schedule • Apprehension with dental procedures and the possibility of pain • Worried about making dental visits a positive experience for her children • Cannot solve several issues with one visit and needs to visit several times
Wishlist	• Establish a regular dental care routine for the whole family • Overcome dental anxiety and feel comfortable during visits • Improve overall oral health and prevent future issues • Save time and reduce stress related to dental appointments

Note

By developing this customer persona, the dental office is able to craft its services and marketing to meet the unique needs and concerns of clients such as Sarah. This is a very strong persona since it represents a big demographic: time-pressed parents who put their family's health first but struggle to fit routine dental care into their own lives. The office may use this information in a more focused approach to acquire and retain patients, using tools such as convenience, anxiolysis, and even family-friendly services.

Notes

1 This is the minimum information required for a customer avatar. It needs to be personalized/adjusted based on the specific situation; see the following sample.
2 You can even add an image/photo of your avatar.

APPENDIX 2
AI prompts for entrepreneurial endeavors

The following prompts are designed to stimulate innovative thinking, strategic planning, and growth for entrepreneurs. These prompts are tailored to address key areas of business development and entrepreneurial success. The prompts can be personalized, and more details can be included to fit your needs.

1. Innovative brainstorming

'Generate 5 disruptive business ideas that leverage emerging technologies such as AI, blockchain, or IoT to solve a significant problem in [your industry]. For each idea, outline its unique value proposition and potential market impact.'

2. Feasibility study

'Conduct a comprehensive feasibility analysis for [your business idea]. Include market size estimates, competitor analysis, required resources, potential risks, and a break-even projection. Provide a SWOT analysis complemented by an action plan and suggest methods for gathering quantitative data to support your findings.'

3. Task optimization

'Analyze the current workflow for [specific business process] and identify inefficiencies. Propose an optimized workflow that incorporates automation and AI technologies where applicable. Estimate the potential time and cost savings of the new process.'

4. Growth strategy

'Develop a 12-month growth strategy for [your business]. Include specific, measurable goals for customer acquisition, revenue growth, and market expansion. Identify key performance indicators (KPIs) and outline the resources needed to achieve these goals.'

5. Strategic planning

'Create a 5-year strategic plan for [your company]. Include vision and mission statements, long-term objectives, and strategies for achieving them. Consider potential market trends, technological advancements, and competitive landscape changes.'

6. Project management

'Design a project management framework for launching [new product/service]. Include a detailed timeline, resource allocation plan, risk mitigation strategies, and key milestones. Specify how you will measure project success and manage stakeholder expectations.'

7. Decision making

'As the founder of a startup facing [specific decision], use the OODA Loop framework to evaluate this choice. First, observe the current situation and market conditions relevant to this decision. Then, orient yourself by analyzing how this aligns with our company's vision, strategic objectives, and core principles. Next, decide on the best course of action, considering both short-term impacts and long-term consequences. Finally, outline an action plan for implementation, including key metrics to track. Also, identify potential risks or challenges we may encounter and how we'll address them. Please provide your reasoning at each step of this process.'

8. Financial planning

'Develop a comprehensive financial model for [your business] for the next 3 years. Include projected income statements, balance sheets, and cash flow statements. Identify key financial ratios to monitor and set specific targets for each.'

9. Market expansion

'Analyze potential new markets for [your product/service]. Identify the top three most promising markets based on factors such as market size, competition, regulatory environment, and alignment with your company's strengths. Outline an entry strategy for each market.'

10. Innovation pipeline

'Create an innovation pipeline for [your company]. Outline a process for generating, evaluating, and implementing new ideas. Include methods for fostering a culture of innovation within your team and metrics for measuring the success of your innovation efforts.'

INDEX

Note: Page numbers in *italics* indicate figures, page numbers in **bold** indicate a table on the corresponding page, and references following "n" refer to notes.

Made in the USA
Monee, IL
13 September 2026

62977120R00105